1,000,000 Books

are available to read at

www.ForgottenBooks.com

Read online
Download PDF
Purchase in print

ISBN 978-1-330-11236-6
PIBN 10028680

This book is a reproduction of an important historical work. Forgotten Books uses state-of-the-art technology to digitally reconstruct the work, preserving the original format whilst repairing imperfections present in the aged copy. In rare cases, an imperfection in the original, such as a blemish or missing page, may be replicated in our edition. We do, however, repair the vast majority of imperfections successfully; any imperfections that remain are intentionally left to preserve the state of such historical works.

Forgotten Books is a registered trademark of FB &c Ltd.
Copyright © 2018 FB &c Ltd.
FB &c Ltd, Dalton House, 60 Windsor Avenue, London, SW19 2RR.
Company number 08720141. Registered in England and Wales.

For support please visit www.forgottenbooks.com

1 MONTH OF FREE READING

at

www.ForgottenBooks.com

By purchasing this book you are eligible for one month membership to ForgottenBooks.com, giving you unlimited access to our entire collection of over 1,000,000 titles via our web site and mobile apps.

To claim your free month visit: www.forgottenbooks.com/free28680

* Offer is valid for 45 days from date of purchase. Terms and conditions apply.

English
Français
Deutsche
Italiano
Español
Português

www.forgottenbooks.com

Mythology Photography **Fiction**
Fishing Christianity **Art** Cooking
Essays Buddhism Freemasonry
Medicine **Biology** Music **Ancient Egypt** Evolution Carpentry Physics
Dance Geology **Mathematics** Fitness
Shakespeare **Folklore** Yoga Marketing
Confidence Immortality Biographies
Poetry **Psychology** Witchcraft
Electronics Chemistry History **Law**
Accounting **Philosophy** Anthropology
Alchemy Drama Quantum Mechanics
Atheism Sexual Health **Ancient History**
Entrepreneurship Languages Sport
Paleontology Needlework Islam
Metaphysics Investment Archaeology
Parenting Statistics Criminology
Motivational

EDITED BY
HORACE G. HUTCHINSON

With Contributions by Specialists in dealing with the different types of Soils on which Golf is played in Great Britain

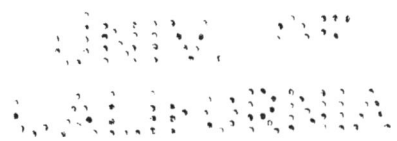

PUBLISHED AT THE OFFICES OF "COUNTRY LIFE," Ltd. TAVISTOCK STREET, COVENT GARDEN, W.C. & BY GEORGE NEWNES, Ltd. SOUTHAMPTON STREET, STRAND, W.C.
CHARLES SCRIBNERS' SONS   MCMVI

GV965
H7

CONTENTS

CHAP.		PAGE.
1.	Introductory, by Horace G. Hutchinson	9
2.	The Formation of Turf, by Gilbert Beale (Messrs. Carter)	19
3.	Treatment and Upkeep of Seaside Links, by Hugh Hamilton	46
4.	Typical East Coast Links — Deal, by Henry Hunter	59
5.	Treatment and Upkeep of a Golf Course on Light Inland Soil, by H. S. Colt	62
6.	Construction and Upkeep of Heath Land Courses, by W. Herbert Fowler	91
7.	Formation and Upkeep of Courses made out of Pine Forests, by S. Mure Fergusson	119
8.	Treatment of an Inland Green on Medium Soil, by Peter Lees	127
9.	Upkeep of a Golf Course on Chalk Downs, by Leonard Keyser	134
10.	Golf Course on Heavy Soil, by James Braid	142
11.	Making a Park Course, by E. Mepham	147
12.	Formation and Placing of Hazards, by C. K. Hutchison	155
13.	Remarks on the Laying Out of Courses, by H. H. Hilton	163
14.	The Championship Courses, by H. H. Hilton	172
15.	General Deductions on Greenkeeping, by Horace G. Hutchinson	194
16.	A Few Leading Principles in Laying Out Links, by Horace G. Hutchinson	208

CHAPTER I

INTRODUCTORY

By HORACE G. HUTCHINSON

THE object of this book is to help the Green Committees, greenkeepers, and all who have to do with the formation and upkeep of golf links and courses. Not very many years ago it used to be said and thought that golf, in the proper sense of the game, could not be played, or certainly could not be enjoyed, anywhere except at the seaside, on soil of that formation which is specially called links. Links is always, so far as I have seen, ground made by what a golfer, who had that little knowledge which is such a " dangerous thing," called " adipose deposit." He meant " alluvial deposit." This alluvial deposit, as is well known, is formed by the debouchment of a river into the sea, and the silting up of sand as the tides meet the river's outflow. Then the winds blow more sand into heaps, marram grass grows on the heaps and binds them together, and thus, as the wise geologists tell us, Providence made golf links for the use of man. This is the kind of links that has been made at St. Andrews, Carnoustie,

Montrose, Peterhead, Nairn, North Berwick, and all along the Forth, Sandwich, Bembridge, Aldeburgh, Westward Ho, Aberdovey, Harlech, Hoylake, and plenty more. It is no use naming them all; but at all, so far as I know, that have the real links characteristics, there is evidence that the sea and a river have been at work together to produce them. Some years ago, as I say, we used to think that we could not play golf on ground of any other kind, and this although the golf club of Blackheath is the oldest establishment of its kind known to history, and although one of the Perth clubs dates back to 1824. The Perth ground, however, formed by the silting of the great river, remote though it is from the sea, has a measure of likeness with the real links soil. We seem to see a formation of rather a like kind in the two Richmond greens. As for Blackheath, that was accepted frankly as a substitute, the best that could be obtained, so far from the sea, for the real thing.

If we had never departed from the view that golf was good only by the sea, it would not have been any use to collect all this book of wisdom. But, happily, we have ceased to be so exclusive, and almost of necessity, for if all the golfers of to-day were to insist on playing by the seaside, they would jostle each other into the waves. We have learned that golf can be played on inland soils, and in course of learning that lesson we have, in the passage of the last fifteen years, been learning a great deal about the best manner of preparing these inland soils to make the golf that we play on them as good, and as like the real seaside thing, as possible. The seaside did not want so much help from art in order to be useful to the golfer as the inland soil. On some links he had but to cut a hole, and he could start and play forthwith. Westward Ho at its commencement was of this happy constitution. Heavier soils required much more preparation, and by the time the golfer of the inland greens had succeeded in bringing them up to a certain state of imperfection, his views as to what was wanted for a golf course had been educated. He began to demand more, even of his seaside links, so that tees had to be levelled, putting greens had to be extended, and so on, to meet his cultured tastes. However, the lesson began to be learned that putting greens, even on seaside links, do not go on recuperating their vigour for ever, so that the golfer may go on putting on them and never give them back any care in return. Some of our most splendid links—St. Andrews and Hoylake are examples — had a moment in their history when the putting greens were parlous bad. I fear, from what I hear, that others of the best are going through that bad time even now. But in the process of these years we have learnt not only that greens require care, but also the kind of care that they require. These have been years of empiricism, of experiment, of failure leading to success. Lessons have been learnt in these years. One of the lessons is that different courses require very different treatment—different because their soil is different, their climate is different, they differ in the circumstances of the amount of play on them: it makes a difference whether they are surrounded with lands that are richly tilled, from which the soil and the dressing may blow over them, or whether barren lands or more barren sea are about them; they differ as to their natural grasses.

Therefore, in the endeavour to make this book a complete guide to the greenkeeper, the best authorities, as they have seemed, and authorities with special skill in the management of the various typical greens — greens typical of the chief varieties in soils and climate—have been approached with the object of getting them to give the greenkeeping world the benefit of their knowledge and experience, and this they have very kindly done. There are one or two chapters on either special or general problems connected with the aying-out of courses which are contributed by writers whose names are a guarantee of their efficiency—such as Mr. Hilton and Mr. C. K. Hutchison. Moreover, during all these years in which we have been learning our lessons, chiefly through the painful experience of repeated failure, the scientific and practical seedsmen have been at work experimenting on and studying the problem of greenkeeping and the best grasses to sow, and best way of treating the ground generally. Mr. Beale, partner in Messrs. Carter's, has paid especial attention to the subject, and the golfer will find a chapter by him giving the results of his attention and experiments. I do not think that the old-time golfer—he whose opinion it was that golf could only be played on the seaside green—was conscious that there was more than one kind of grass seed. Grass, like flesh, was grass to him, and that was the end of it, and all talk of fescues and poas he would have regarded as so much rubbish. The advance in requirements of golf greens has proceeded with equal steps with a general advance in gardening knowledge and interest, of which the result is that we know a good deal more than we did about the kind of seed to sow in a particular soil.

The great mistake—I think it is not going too far to give it this notable pre-eminence—that we used to make at first when we began to play golf on inland greens and to work at getting them into what we fondly imagined to be the best possible condition for golf, was in ever rolling the putting greens to an extent that is now hardly credible. We used to roll them with iron rollers, basting down the soil so that no grass could grow through it, no ball would stop on it, and no putting was possible on it. All putting was reduced to trickling, and the golfer who followed the gallant old maxim of "going for the back of the hole" would run nearly off the green unless he caught the back of the hole very fair and square indeed. If we were ever found fault with for this, we used to answer that it was the only way to remove worm-earth and get quit of the inequalities. We have moved a little beyond that very primitive stage now, and it will be observed in the following pages that a strong consensus of opinion is expressed that for the putting greens rolling with light rollers of wood is very much better than rolling with the iron rollers, and that too much rolling even with them is to be depreciated.

The varieties of soil that the golfing greenkeeper may now be called on to deal with are very many, and they range from the lightest of seaside soil to the heaviest of clay. I hope I am not doing an injustice to the fine inland course of Romford in taking it as the type of the heavy courses. At the other end of the range, I take Deal and St. Andrews as typical of seaside courses on the East Coast of England and Scotland respectively, where the drying winds prevail, and where there is not a great deal of moisture. Of the inland soils we cannot go far wrong in taking Sunningdale as a fair type of the lightest, and most similar to the greens by the sea. New Zealand has a soil not very unlike it, but here the original laying-out of the course was beset with a difficulty of rather a special nature in the big fir trees that it was necessary to uproot in order to clear the ground. A soil that is fairly light, though not so light as at Sunningdale, is that of Walton Heath, on which so much labour and care has been spent with such very satisfactory results. Here there is the advantage of natural sand in the bunkers, and the manner in which all its problems have been tackled makes it quite a good object lesson for those who have similar ones to face. My own lessons in the treatment of down courses—courses made out of land where the chalk is very near the surface—were learned at Eastbourne, which is as fairly typical of its kind as can be found, and at Winchester, which is taken as the object lesson in the making of chalk down courses. I presume that the problems were practically identical with those at Eastbourne. That seems so to cover most of the range between the lightest and the heaviest that all of the normal soils within the British Isles are, perhaps, fairly accounted for. Golf on "the barren rocks of Aden" and the wee outlandish places will require a special treatment. "Where all the Greens are Brown," a treatise on upkeep of "browns" would be more in place than this present one. A good many people are interested in laying out courses in their own parks, and, as this is a question of expense falling on the owner, the cost of formation and of maintenance becomes very serious. There the question will be found considered and discussed pretty carefully in the chapter on park courses by a greenkeeper whose experience was gained in a park that has an unusual variety of soil within so small an extent. A point that is always worth remembering in laying out a course of this kind, or wherever expense is a vital question and there is not likely to be a great press of players, is that by a little judicious dodging it is often possible to play the same hole, or one or two of the same holes, twice over, approaching them from different directions, and thus, in each instance, making a single green serve a double purpose, with a cent. per cent. saving in each case both in the first outlay and the current expense of maintenance.

Those who have not much knowledge or experience of golf and its many problems will be perhaps disposed to wonder that so great and splendid a book as this should be needed to collect the stored wisdom relative to its principal topic, but only those of little experience will take such a view. An example of the various answers that the same question requires under various circumstances may be found by considering the care of rabbits, and their work on golf greens. One of the first things that the greenkeeper has to do on very many of the wild places when he begins to set about adapting them for golf is to get rid of the rabbits, and, having reduced their numbers to limits that are reasonable, he has to wage a constant war against

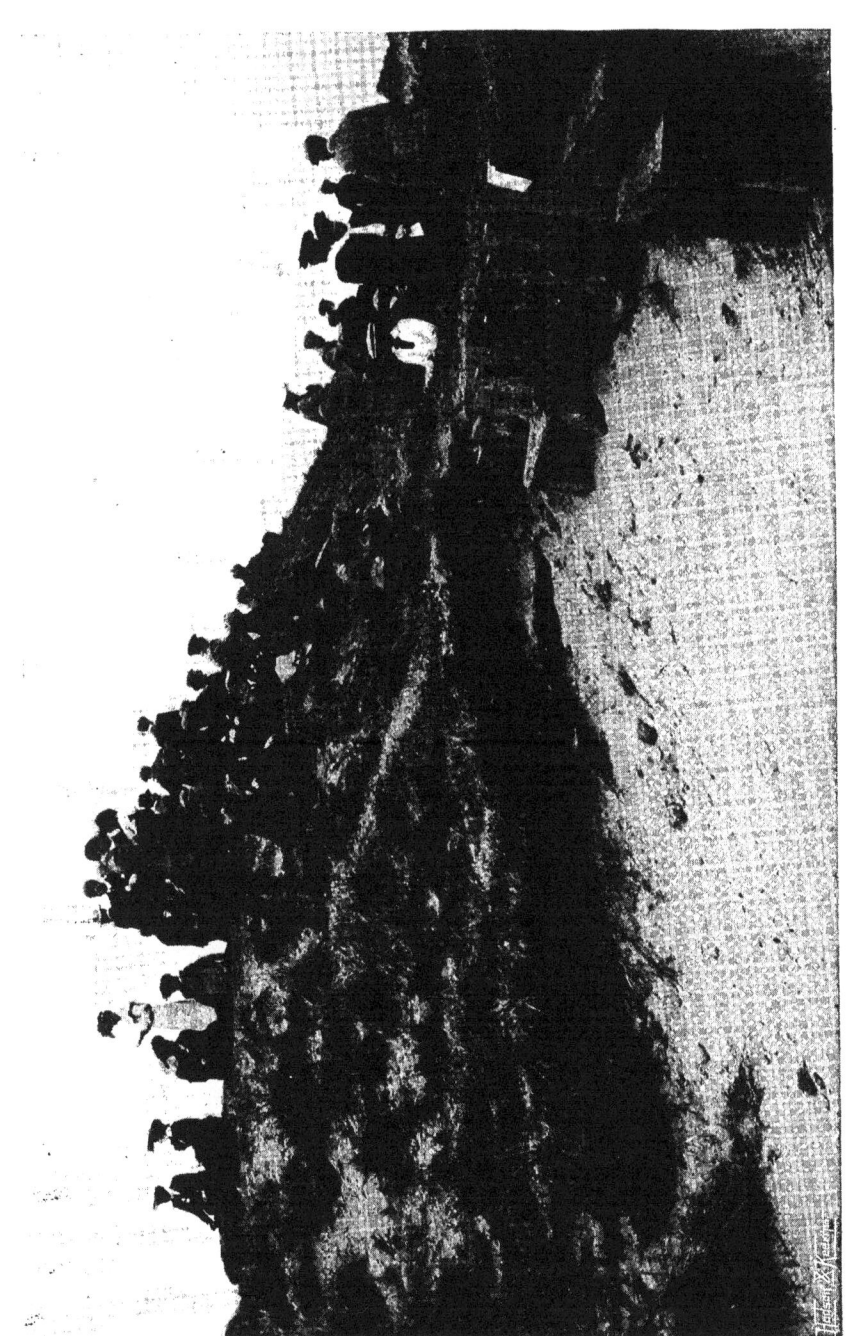

HIGH SAND HILLS GIVE GOOD POINTS OF VIEW.

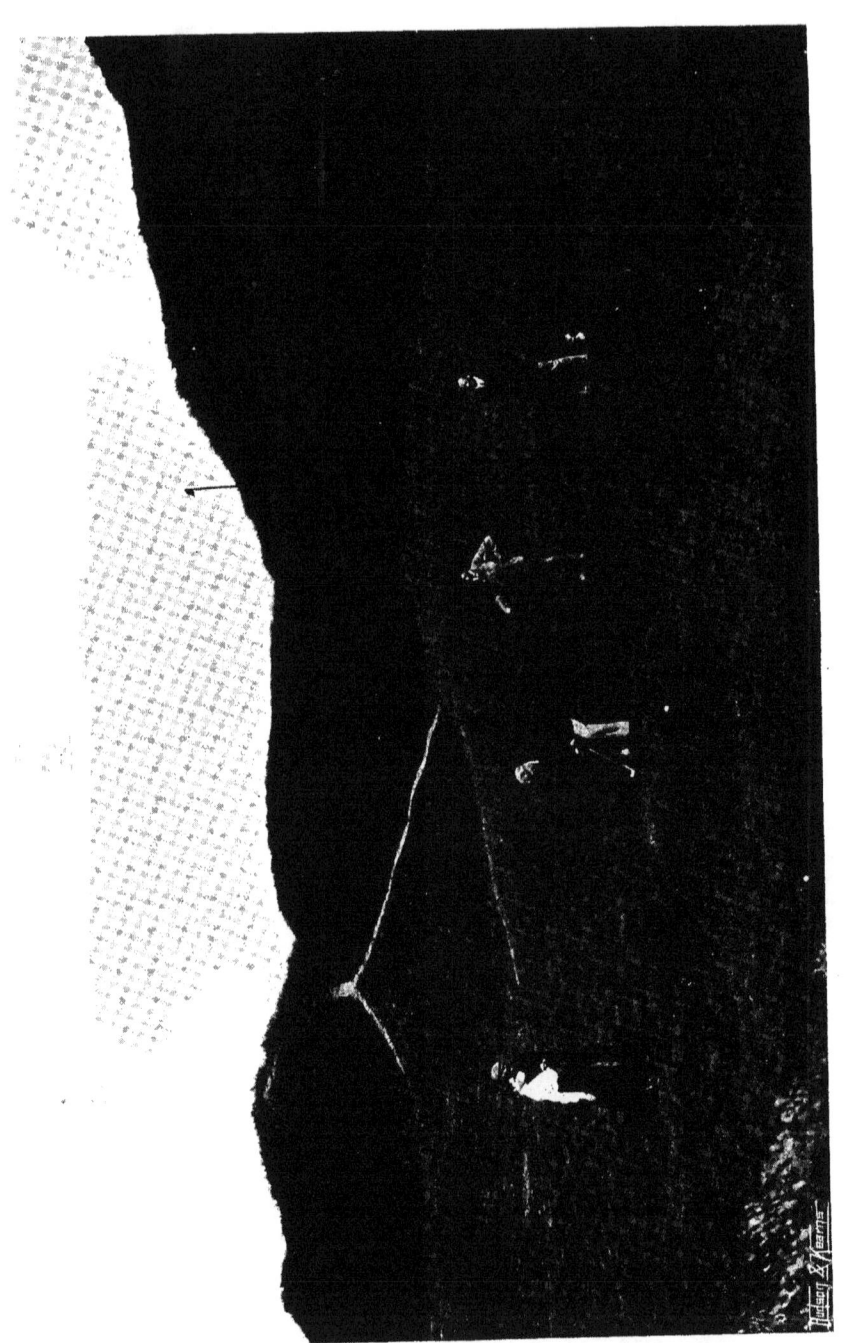

MAIDEN GREEN, SANDWICH.

the processes of nature so as to keep them within those limits of sound reason. Yet there are greens on which the rabbits are the chief, and almost the only, greenkeepers. Notable among these are the greens on the south shore of the Firth of Forth, from North Berwick (not including North Berwick among them, nor Muirfield) to Aberlady. But what would Archerfield, Gullane, Luffness be without their rabbits? The rabbits crop the grass short and produce an admirable quality of springy turf. I do not suppose any other greens are kept up to an equal degree of excellence with so little expense in wages of greenkeepers as these, and all because the rabbits do so much of the work, without payment. The course, no doubt, had to be prepared in the first instance, but it is found that when once the good surface of turf has been made the rabbits do not care much to come and scratch their burrows and little pits — just of the right size for the interment of a golf ball—thereon. They will quickly go to work on any broken ground, and break it more thoroughly, but the perfect sward seems to have no attractions for them; they even seem to take a pride in keeping it unbroken.

Very few instructions in the science and art of greenkeeping can be of real use if they are given in general terms. Each case, each variety of soil, has to be treated according to special characteristics: what is one soil's meat is another soil's poison, and even the same soils require very different treatment in different climates. These differences do not seem to me to have been at all sufficiently appreciated hitherto, and much of our failure has been due to the unthinking adoption of methods, which have been found good on one green, by the keeper of another which has quite a different kind of soil. I have tried to choose as object lessons the courses most typical of the different kinds, and the men whose experience has been gained on those courses and who have made them their special study have been kind enough to give generously of their experience; and I am in hopes that when any greenkeeper takes up the book and tries to find in it instruction or hints for dealing with the soil in which he is particularly interested, he will not, speaking of British golf, look in vain. If there are any big gaps or notable omissions both publisher and editor would be much obliged if they were pointed out.

CHAPTER II

THE FORMATION OF TURF

By Mr. GILBERT BEALE (*partner in Messrs. Carter, Seedsmen, High Holborn*)

FAIR American admiring the really wonderful lawns at one of the Universities—

"Say, gardener, how do you make a lawn like this?"

Gardener—"Well, miss, we rolls 'em and mows 'em and rolls 'em and mows 'em for 300 years."

Confusion of the fair American!

This ancient joke seems, on the face of it, to be rather far-fetched, but when one realises that until a few years back it was recognised by all that a new lawn or green could not be made, if sown with grass seed, in less than three years, and that this belief is still rigidly adhered to by many, Mr. Punch, the perpetrator of the joke, must be justly and fully exonerated.

But why did it take at least three years to make a lawn? For the simple reason that the grass seed was sown so thinly (from three to four bushels per acre), that each plant had to grow to its full size before the ground was covered.

This slow process suited its time, but now the strenuous life demands quicker results, and, by a series of experiments, not only have several new or improved varieties of grasses been found, which tiller out over the ground instead of growing in tufts, as the older varieties did, but by judiciously increasing the amount of seed sown per acre, according to the fineness of the mixture, the quality of the soil, and the time in which the ground is required for play, a lawn or green can be and has been made with a close, uniform, and even turf, fit for play in from about nine to twelve months from the time the seed was sown.

I have seen greens and entire golf courses grown in eight months, and not only was the turf strong enough for regular play, but it had the appearance and bottom of a good, old turf, such as is found at the seaside and in some of our famous parks; and I have actually seen Willie Park, of Huntercombe, superintending the turfing of a golf green with turf only six months old. The seed was sown late in October and the turf was cut and laid in the following April.

I will now try to explain as concisely as possible the method which should be employed for procuring a turf in the shortest possible period of time.

When making a new lawn or green, commence the work as soon as possible after the break up of the hot summer weather, with the intention of sowing, if possible, at the end of

August or during the early days of September. The soil is warm at the end of summer, and an abundance of rain and dew may be expected, which is very beneficial to the growth of the seed, and the young grass will have ample time to become well established before the real cold weather sets in. And, as weeds are far more in evidence in the spring than they are in the summer, it follows that the long start given to the autumn-sown grass should make it better able to withstand the onslaught of any weeds that may be lying dormant in the soil when they appear in the spring.

For spring sowing, prepare the ground as soon as the weather permits, and sow the seed (again weather permitting) early in March; or, should it be a severe season, delay sowing until the early days of April.

It is always a good policy to allow as much time as possible in which to prepare the ground. A month or six weeks is not too much, as the surface will, to a certain extent, find its own level, which can more easily be corrected before than after the seed is sown. When the work is done in a hurry it is generally badly done, as it gives no chance for the surface to consolidate (which is so essential for the welfare of the young grass plants), or for quick-growing weeds to assert themselves and be destroyed before the grass seeds are sown. A lawn made under the modern system, if autumn-sown, that is, during

August or early in September, should be fit for play before the end of the summer; if spring-sown, that is, during March or early in April, should be fit for play by the end of the summer. These results cannot be obtained if old-fashioned, parsimonious methods are adopted, and to obtain these results the ground must be liberally treated and prepared in the following manner:—

Dig to a depth of a spade, turn the soil well over, break up the large clods, pick out all large stones, weeds, roots, etc. The fact that grass is a shallow-rooted plant makes it quite unnecessary to work the soil to a greater depth unless the old turf is to be buried. In that case the surface should be turned under to a depth of two spades. Work into the soil a generous quantity of manure. This is an important operation, and one that is generally omitted altogether or is badly carried out. The best general manures are peat-moss, stable litter, old, well-rotted short straw, and artificials. In all cases spread the manure over the surface and fork it in to a depth of from three to six inches; in this way its fullest benefits are kept near to the surface and within easy reach of the roots of the grass. Prepare the seed-bed by breaking up the clods, removing large stones and all weed roots with an iron-toothed rake; roll and cross-roll the ground with a light roller until the surface is perfectly hard and, when walked on, hardly shows the imprint of the foot. It will then be ready to receive the seed. Sow the seed on a calm, dry day, otherwise much of the seed may be blown away and lost, or, should the soil be wet, it will stick to the operator's boots, and in this way the level may be seriously disturbed. Slightly stir the surface with a rake, and divide up the ground into strips about three feet wide by means of pegs and string, and divide the seed into as many equal portions as there are strips or squares; this will be found an easy way to ensure an even distribution of the seed. Sow the seed by hand, with the back bent, taking care to spread it as evenly as possible over the surface. The seed must now be covered to a depth not exceeding a quarter of an inch, otherwise much of it will be lost. There are two ways of doing this, the most simple being to lightly rake the surface in two directions, taking care not to bury the seed too deeply. This is the method adopted by most professional gardeners. Another way is to cover the seed with light, sifted soil, as free from weed seeds as possible. A skilled man can very quickly cover a fair-sized lawn by scattering the sifted soil with a shovel. People who are not adepts at this may carry the sifted soil in a pail and scatter it over the surface by hand. After levelling with a rake, the whole should be lightly rolled down. Under favourable conditions the young grass will appear above the ground from fourteen to twenty-one days after sowing, according to the weather. When about one and a half to two inches high, it is ready to be cut. It is necessary for the welfare of the young spears to cut them with a scythe the first two or three times, so as to enable the roots to become sufficiently strong to be able to resist the slight snatching movement of a machine, which can then be used with safety. Any thin or bare places should be repaired as soon as noticed, by very carefully loosening the surface soil, sowing a handful of seed, covering and rolling in the usual manner. The lawn should be rolled with a light roller after the grass is cut for the first time or two, and is thus gradually got into condition for play. A worn or poor turf is usually the result of hard usage, poverty of soil, or want of proper drainage. The result of hard usage is shown by the appearance of bare patches; the trade mark of a poor soil is a thin turf and bare patches, with moss and an increasing number of weeds; while moss and stagnant water usually denote faulty drainage.

As weeds and drainage are rather important subjects they will be dealt with separately, and we will now presume that the lawn is suffering from hard wear or poverty of soil. In both cases the remedy is the same: mow the lawn with a mowing machine, cutting the grass as short as possible, then rake and cross-rake the surface with an iron-toothed rake, taking care to thoroughly open up the surface. It is well to remember that

GENERAL VIEW OF SUNNINGDALE.

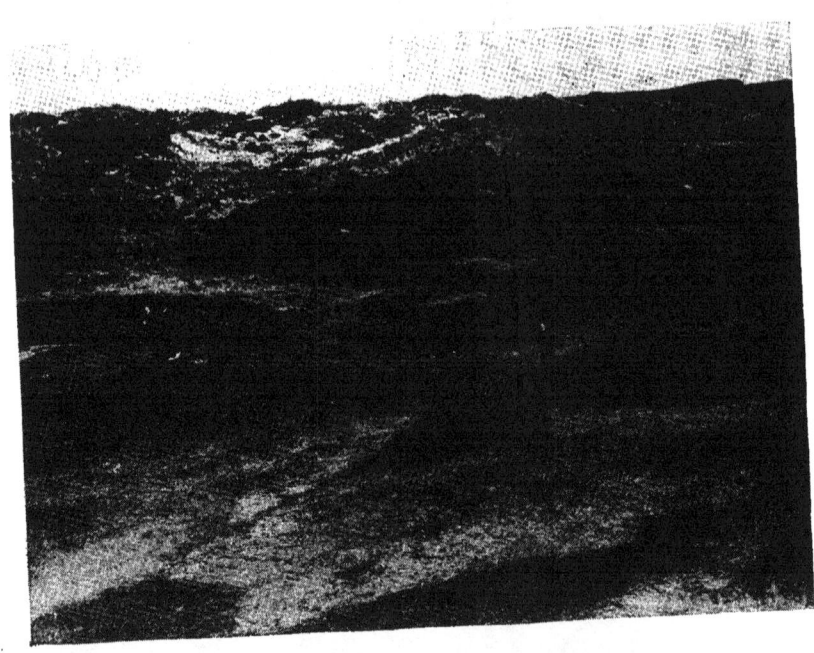

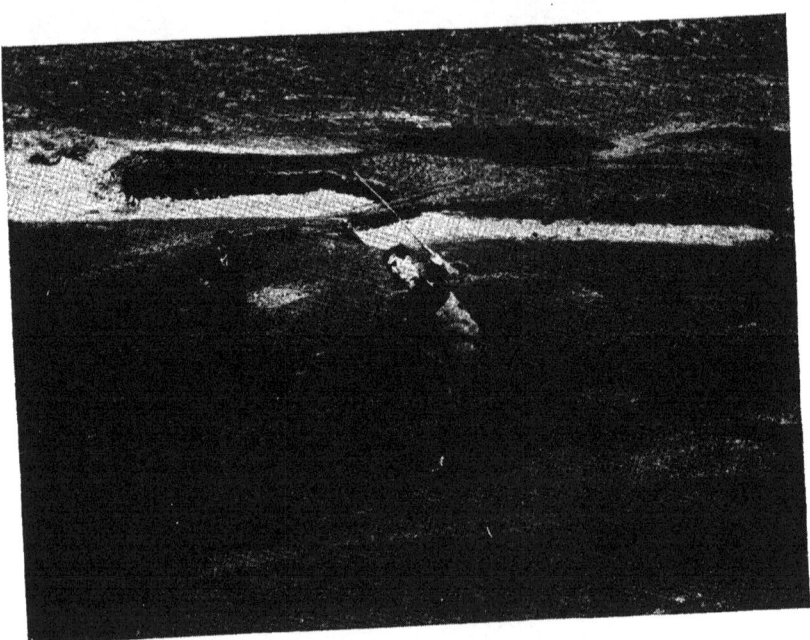

VIEWS OF FORMBY LINKS

the more the existing plant appears to be ruined, short of actually pulling it out by the roots, the better will be the results; and that unless the surface is loosened sufficiently, the roots of the young grass will not be able to penetrate the old turf, and consequently they will die, and the whole work prove a failure. There are now two ways of completing the work, the first being to sow the seed on a raked surface, choosing a dry day, otherwise a quantity of the seed will stick to the wet leaves of the existing plant and so perish. If the raking has been carried out well, the surface will present a multitude of little furrows, which will receive the seed and make excellent seed-beds. Sow the seed thickly or thinly according to the state of the turf. Cover the seed with prepared soil or compost either by scattering it with a shovel or by hand. The alternative is to scatter prepared soil over the area under treatment before sowing the seed, then to sow and cover in the usual manner, the finishing touch being given with a light roller, which should be drawn over the lawn in two different directions.

It is very simple to keep a lawn in good condition, although it entails a certain amount of expense and constant work. If a lawn is not kept up to the mark it is sure to deteriorate: the weeds will multiply, the soil become more poverty-stricken, and eventually it will have to be either re-sown or renovated. In fact, all lawns or greens should be top-dressed at least once a year with a good artificial manure or prepared compost, the best season of application being between September and October, or March and April. It is also most important to frequently roll the grass with a light roller, and to keep it closely cut, using a good machine, which must be kept in good running order.

Lastly, the weeds must be reduced or exterminated, otherwise they will increase, and it is impossible for a lawn to be termed good when it is infested with weeds.

Drainage is rather a comprehensive subject, and one that cannot be treated lightly, and these notes should only be used as a base upon which to formulate a scheme to suit the particular case under consideration, as it is quite impossible to make hard and fast rules to suit all situations and formations of soils. Land drain-pipes are perhaps the most popular for draining a lawn, and these should be laid in herring-bone formation, using 4-inch piping for the main drain and 2- to 3-inch for the subsidiary drains. The pipes should be laid in trenches from twelve to twenty-four inches deep, the subsidiary drains being about ten to fifteen feet apart, and entering the main drain at an angle of over 45 degrees, so as not to arrest the flow of the water. It is advisable to set the joints in cement in the vicinity of shrubs or trees, otherwise their roots will enter the drain and possibly choke it; also, partly to fill the trenches with clinkers or other porous material, as this will be found to increase the effectiveness of the drain, especially in clayey land. The depth of the drain, the size of the pipes, and distance apart, being entirely dependent upon the character of the soil and general local conditions, must be decided by the person doing the work. Draining by means of pipes should be completed several months before any attempt is made to sow grass seed, as the soil in the trenches is bound to sink to a certain extent, and unless this can be corrected before the lawn is finished, it is likely to give an unsightly appearance.

Another and very effective way of draining a small lawn is to sink a vertical shaft about four feet square in the centre of a level lawn, or at the lowest part of an uneven lawn or putting green, with the object of penetrating, if possible, into porous strata. Here local knowledge must again come into play. Generally speaking, one is pretty sure to strike something suitable at a depth of ten or fifteen feet. Fill the shaft with large stones or clinkers, building them in carefully and firmly, so as to leave as much room as possible for the water. From the shaft to the outskirts of the lawn cut four more trenches, being twelve to fifteen inches deep at the extreme end, about two feet six inches at the shaft end. In these lay 3-inch drain-pipes, taking care to protect the shaft ends with large stones. Fill up the trenches and the top of the shaft with porous soil, and the work is complete. In the case of striking heavy clay, an effort should be made to penetrate it; but should this prove to be too difficult, make a good deep shaft, fill up the bottom with old tin cans, pails, etc., and finish off with stones in the above manner. A shaft such as this will be found to be fairly effective.

Another method is to reach the porous strata by means of a boring tool. The plant consists of a pair of shears or tripod, a pulley wheel, and a boring tool to be turned by hand. With these a lawn can be drained without doing it any damage at all. Make a wooden platform about six feet square, with a hole cut in the centre large enough to take the boring tool. Erect the shears and pulley wheel over this. You now take the boring tool, which is for all the world like a large gimlet, and twist it into the earth, pulling it out every few minutes by means of the wheel so as to remove the loosened soil. By this means it is quite easy to sink drains to a depth of twenty or thirty feet. The wooden platform takes all the wear and dirt, and so prevents the work from injuring the turf. The number of drains required to be constructed in this way would depend upon the tenacity of the soil, but as a rule ten feet apart would be found a useful distance. The drains can be finished by either filling them to within a foot of the surface with shingle or else by lining them with drain pipes. If the latter method be chosen, the pipes must be lowered into position carefully, otherwise they will break. The best way to do this is to take a piece of wood slightly longer than the diameter of the pipe, to the centre of the stick fix a strong piece of cord, thread the pipes upon the cord, and lower into position. Finish off the drain by placing an inverted flower pot over it, and filling up the remaining distance with porous soil.

When a level surface is required, all small irregularities should be corrected when digging and preparing the ground, and a level tee or green can be made on a slope by taking soil from the high ground and placing it upon the low ground. On a deep soil this is very simple. In many cases where the soil is not very deep, a level surface can be obtained by employing imported soil, but the bottom should always be loosened up first of all. When soil is imported for the purpose, and it is of uniform quality, it can be shot down where needed, and trodden down firmly, the surface being made even as the work proceeds; but, on the other hand, if the brought soil is of different qualities, it must be spread over in layers, keeping the stiff soil at the bottom and the more friable on the surface. It is not advisable to go to the expense of work of this kind unless one is prepared to put at least six or eight inches of good light soil upon the surface. The usual method employed in levelling land is to drive stout pegs into the soil at equal distances, let us say six feet apart (these pegs can be accurately adjusted by means of a spirit level); the soil is then made up to the level of the pegs. It is always advisable to allow made-up land to stand some time before seeding, as it is pretty certain to settle in places, and the intervening time can be profitably occupied by correcting the level, freeing the land from weeds, and enriching the soil. To correct the level of established turf, carefully remove the turf with a turfing iron, add or remove soil as is necessary, and replace the turf.

Manures must be divided into two parts, viz., manures for digging or ploughing into freshly broken ground, and manures or composts for top-dressing existing lawns or greens with the object of improving them. When preparing ground for golf the majority of people will not see the importance of enriching the soil before sowing the seed. Several reasons are presented why the land should not be manured. It is either in good heart, or it appears to be, etc., etc. But I present one, and only one, why land should be manured. It is this: when once a lawn is formed the turf has to obtain the larger share of its nourishment from a few inches of surface soil, possibly for ever. The soil cannot again be disturbed, consequently it does not get ameliorated by the action of air, rain, or frost to the same extent as tilled land, which is continually being turned over, or relieved by a change of crop; and the grasses which form a turf are just as liable to suffer from starvation as anything else. When preparing ground for a lawn, however good the soil may appear to be, make assurance doubly sure by working into the surface one load of well-rotted straw manure to every 100 yards on heavy soils, and a similar quantity of stable peat-litter on light soils. These quantities can be increased with advantage should the soil be poor and the turf likely to be subjected to hard wear.

Top-dressing manures and composts consist of prepared and unprepared composts. The former consists of stable or farm manure, fresh or old, which has been mixed with all or any of the following soils: leaf mould, night soil, old, rotten turf, old potting soil, old hotbeds, wood ashes, etc., and has been allowed to stand in a heap for some time, and has been turned over at least once or twice during that time.

This compost should be chopped up before use with a spade and thrown through a $\frac{1}{4}$-inch straight-wire sand screen, and applied by scattering it with a shovel over the lawn any time of the year with the exception of summer. The fine dressing produced and used in this way can be brushed in with a birch broom or bush harrow, or, if left to the weather, will disappear from sight after the first rain-shower, and so prevents the unsightly appearance of a lawn covered with clods.

Unprepared dressings may also be applied any time throughout the year, with the exception of the summer months, and consist of leaf mould, old potting soil, rotten turf, old hotbeds, wood ashes, etc., sifted and scattered in the usual way. By this means the turf is sure to benefit, and the garden is rid of certain unsightly heaps. Always turn over the heaps of soil several times before use, and sift top-dressings before spreading them on the lawn, if only to lengthen the life of the mowing machine. It is good policy to give a weedy or mossy lawn a thorough raking before applying the top-dressing. Sea-sand is frequently used as a dressing for putting greens resting upon stiff soils, with the twofold object of firming-up the surface and fining-down a too vigorous growth of grass. The sand must be applied with judgment, otherwise the grass may be smothered, and to reap its full benefits the worms must be killed before it is applied, or they will quickly cover it with their casts, and no lasting improvement will be obtained. It is not advisable to use sand on poor, hungry soils. Clay is rarely used for top-dressing lawns or greens, although "Nottingham marl" is frequently used for top-dressing cricket pitches to enable them to resist the pounding and hard wear to which they are subjected. Artificial manures require careful handling. They do not act equally on all soils, and unless one quite understands what the manure consists of, and whether it is suitable for lawns, it is quite possible to get a very different result from that anticipated. The following is a case in point. A greenkeeper was advised to dress his greens with bone dust, which he did. Before he applied the bone dust they were practically free from clover, but after the first application it at once asserted itself, and quickly overpowered the grass, greatly to the annoyance and wonderment of the man, who unknowingly had supplied the clover with just the food most suitable for its constitution.

It should always be remembered that the "grass" referred to in text books on manures is always grass as found in pastures or for hay, not lawn grass, and as coarse grasses and clovers are very valuable in hay fields and pastures, it is quite easy to see how a mistake can be made. An amateur should apply only such composts or artificials as are prepared by experts.

It is most important that a ground devoted to grasses should be sown with a mixture of grass seeds that is particularly suited to its geological structure. Consequently I strongly advise those in authority to call in an expert to examine the soil, the grasses natural to the district, etc., etc., before buying the seed, so that a prescription of grasses can be procured which is specially prepared to suit the soil, situation, and the purpose for which it is required. No doubt it will surprise many people to know that there are scores of different varieties of grasses, and that each variety or group thrives best when planted in a favourable situation and in soil suited to its constitution and habit. Clover should never be added to these prescriptions unless for some special reason. A small quantity of clover is not objectionable in a pleasure lawn, but it is a positive nuisance in a lawn devoted to games, as it gives a patchy appearance to the turf. It is slippery and becomes pulped under hard wear, it holds dew longer than grass, and it discolours the balls.

All the finest growing grasses that are most suitable for the formation of a lawn are very shy seeders: that is, when grown for seed, they yield less weight per acre, as is only natural, than do the coarser-growing varieties. Consequently the cheaper the mixture the coarser the turf. But I maintain that the finest dwarf-growing grasses are the most economical in the end, especially when used for sowing-down large areas, as the turf formed by the dwarf, compact habit of the finest grasses requires to be mown only about half as many times as a turf formed by coarser-growing grasses. It would be interesting to compare the mowing bill of a good seaside golf links, or Walton Heath, with that of an ordinary inland links. This is a most important point, especially when one takes into account the large sums of money annually spent on mowing, and an independent investigation would undoubtedly prove that my method of sowing-down land with the finest grasses gives the best results and is the most economical.

Young grass should be cut for the first time, when it is about two inches high, with a sharp scythe. For safety's sake it is advisable to cut it once or twice more with a scythe, so as to allow the young plants to become sufficiently strong to resist the slight pull of the mowing machine. Never allow the grass, whether it be young or old, to grow long and ragged. Two inches may be considered the extreme length to which it should attain at any time of the year. It is not advisable to keep grass too closely cut during hot and dry weather.

If a lawn be free from weeds and is kept closely cut, the machine can be used without the box. The cut grass will not be very noticeable, and will afford the roots of the grass a certain amount of protection during hot and dry weather. This must not be practised on weedy lawns, as the machine would cut off and scatter the weed seeds all over the lawn; whereas, were they collected in the box, together with the cut grass, they would be removed and destroyed.

All go-ahead clubs should have a turf nursery, which is made and used as follows:—Prepare two plots of ground, sow them down, and keep them in exactly the same way as the greens are kept. They will make two pieces of excellent turf, which will be found very useful during the autumn or spring for repairing bare or weak places in the greens. When one plot is cleared, level it up and sow it again, and use the second plot. In this way a continual supply is available at very little cost during all seasons.

Grass will not thrive on a loose surface. After the grass has been cut for the first time, the whole surface must be carefully rolled with a light roller. This should be repeated after each cutting until the turf is strong enough to bear a heavier implement. Do not roll always in the same direction: roll from north to south one day and from east to west the next, and so on. Do not roll when the ground is hard and dry, as it will do no good, or during frosty weather, when it will do serious damage, but roll frequently during the spring and autumn. A wooden roller made up of five 1-foot segments will be found a useful tool for land that requires frequent rolling, such as putting greens, tennis and croquet courts. The best metal rollers are made with two cylinders to facilitate turning, and the outside edges are rounded to prevent them from cutting the turf.

Moss is a sure sign that the soil is out of condition, and is generally caused by poverty or the want of proper drainage. It is generally safe and always less expensive to assume that it is caused by poverty, and to eradicate it by following the directions on renovating, unless there is very strong evidence to the contrary, when it will become necessary to follow the more expensive directions on drainage. Very frequently freshly dug and imported soil will produce a strong crop of weeds, both annual and perennial. How the weeds get into the soil, and how long they will retain their germinating power is a debatable matter into which it is not necessary for me to enter. Darwin tells us that seeds which germinated freely have been found in the little chamber at the end of a worm hole at a depth of eight feet. In his opinion these seeds were taken down the hole by the worms, with the object of lining the little chamber in which they winter in a dormant condition, so as to prevent their skins, through which they breathe, from coming into contact with the cold, damp soil.

There are a multitude of different ways in which weed seeds get into the ground, and the only way of making a good turf upon foul ground is to allow it to lie fallow, and clean it by frequently disturbing the surface with a hoe for a small plot and a harrow for a larger area.

The question of weeds is a very difficult one to handle, and to be at all clear must be divided into two parts, viz., cleaning freshly broken ground and cleaning existing turf.

I always advise my friends to prepare the ground for a new lawn or green as long before the next seeding season as possible. This not only improves the soil and allows it to become consolidated naturally, but it gives an opportunity which should not be lost of freeing the land of the majority of the weeds that it may contain. As soon as the weeds appear, hoe them down, but do not hoe deeply, as this will bring to the surface weed seeds which otherwise would be buried too deeply to grow. When the turf is once formed, any annual weeds that may have escaped the hoeing will be extirpated by the mowing machine, so we can dismiss them from our minds. This leaves the perennial weeds, which may be divided into three classes, as follows :—

> (1.) Weeds with a long tap root, such as dandelions, docks, and certain of the rib grasses.
> (2.) Weeds with roots like a tassel, such as plantains, hawkweed, etc.
> (3.) Weeds which travel above or below the surface, throwing out new roots and growth every few inches, such as daisies, yarrow, and some of the clovers.

I cannot impress upon the minds of my readers too strongly the advisability of weeding systematically. Divide the turf into strips about three feet wide by means of string and pegs, and thoroughly clean one strip before going on to another. It is almost incredible how quickly a lawn can be freed from weeds in this manner.

FORMATION OF TURF

Meandering about a lawn with a spud in one hand and a basket in the other is a laborious and ineffective way of weeding a lawn, as a number of weeds are bound to be missed. The best way to tackle the tap-rooted weeds is to divide the lawn into strips about three feet wide; take a basket to hold the weeds, and a border fork with four flat prongs. Now, to remove the weed successfully, it is necessary to guess the depth of the root. Well-grown dandelions and docks will go down over a foot, the smaller ones and the rib grass about six inches. In the first case, force the fork into the turf as deep as it will go, and as far from the weed as the length of the prongs. By depressing the handle of the fork the turf will be forced up like a mole-hill. If the distance has been guessed correctly it will crack on either side of the weed, which can then be removed easily. In the case of the smaller weeds, force the fork into the soil about six inches deep, and go on as before. After a little practice it is possible to take out weed after weed without leaving behind any of the root, which, if left, might grow again. It is best to weed in this fashion when the soil is damp. Before rolling down the "mole-hills" drop a pinch of seed into the holes left by the weed. Forking up the turf in this way tends to improve it. Removing the crown of a tap-rooted weed with a knife does more harm than good, as in most cases the weed will throw out several crowns to replace the one cut off. Always burn weeds: then you know for certain that they cannot give any more trouble.

Tassel-rooted weeds may be removed in the following way:—Divide up the lawn as before, and take up your position, seated on a low stool about eight or nine inches high, with your legs well forward and apart, so that you can work in between them. Remove the weeds by forcing into the soil a 1-inch chisel (this is by far the most effective tool to use), about one and a half to two inches away from the weed, and about the same depth. By depressing the handle of the chisel the soil will be forced up into a little mound. Take the weed with the left hand, give it a slight shake, and out it comes. When all the weeds in reach have been removed, by placing the right hand on the turf your weight can be removed from the stool, which is then pulled forward by the left hand. Finish off each strip by sprinkling seed into the holes and rolling down. Burn the weeds.

Creeping weeds are by far the most difficult to exterminate, as in most cases a portion of the root left in the soil will grow freely, and it is most difficult to remove entirely a weed of this class in a thick turf. The most successful means I have employed up to date is a preparation called "weed crystal," which is used as follows: For small isolated weeds place a thimbleful of the preparation on the crown of each weed. For large clumps of daisies sprinkle the clump liberally with the preparation on a dry day, so that the whole force of the killer eats into the crown. This preparation, which is really a manure beneficial to grasses, when applied in this manner, will in a few days scorch up and kill the weeds, and when by the action of the weather it loses its potency, it will, unless the clump of weeds was very large, stimulate the surrounding grass to such an extent that the scar left by the weed will quickly disappear. The preparation will also kill other weeds if used as follows :—Cut off the crown of the weed about one inch from the surface, and place a pinch of weed crystal upon the stump. Although this is very effective, I cannot see that it has any advantage over removing the weeds by hand. Clovers and grasses obtain their nourishment from different constituents of the soil, consequently a turf containing clover and other fleshy plants can be quickly improved if dressed with a nitrogenous manure. A lawn infested with creeping weeds can be improved to a very large extent by raking it thoroughly during the spring or autumn with an iron-toothed rake. The action of the rake will break up and tear out a large quantity of weeds, which should be collected and destroyed, especially if the raking is done in two different directions. A lawn subjected to this treatment should always be seeded where necessary, and top-dressed. It is not always good to water young grass before it has become firmly established, as the force of the water, either from a hose or watering-can, disturbs the soil and damages the young and tender plants. If the seed is sown at the right time, that is, as soon as possible after the break-up of the summer (say early September), or spring (say, during March), it may not be found necessary to water it until it is amply strong enough to be able to withstand it, but one should always remember that drought is the worst enemy of young grass plants: a week of hot, dry weather will do ten times as much harm as a month of frost.

Water established turf with a hose or watering-can fitted with a fine rose. Distribute the water evenly over the lawn, giving it sufficient to go down to a depth of six inches. Water late in the afternoon, or, better still, in the evening. Do not water under a hot sun, as it will quickly evaporate, and cause the soil to bake. A lawn that has been regularly watered during the summer should be top-dressed in the autumn.

Fairy rings are caused by a fungoid growth, the spores of which may have been deposited on the lawn by the wind. The mycelium spreads underneath the turf, and, as it exhausts the constituents of the soil which are necessary for its existence, it expands on all sides, as a ring does over the surface of a pond which has been caused by the impact of a stone with the water. As the outside edge of the ring flourishes, the inside decays. This charges the soil with nitrogenous

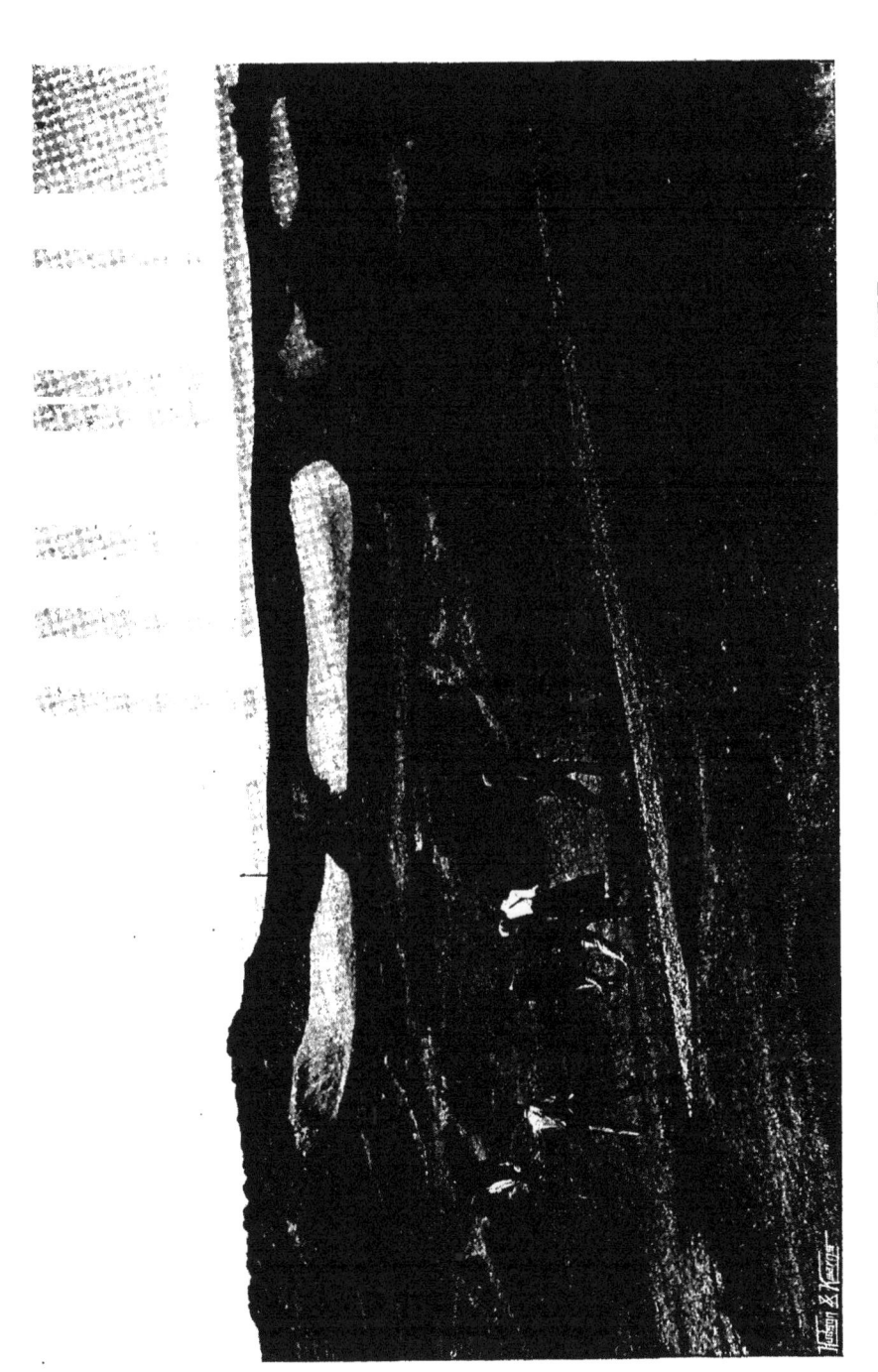

BUNKERS AT SANDWICH FOR THE CARRY FROM 7th TEE.

BURNHAM, SOMERSETSHIRE.

matter, and causes the grass to assume a very dark green colour. As far as I know, the only cure for fairy rings is to remove them bodily, burn the earth taken out, and fill in with fresh material. When removing a fairy ring, do it properly. Cut the turf and soil well away from either side of the ring, making the trench from eighteen to twenty-four inches wide, and about the same depth. As the fungus gives out a very offensive smell, by occasionally smelling a handful of soil one can readily tell if it is necessary to remove any more soil. Give the sides and bottom of the trench a liberal dusting with quicklime, allow the trenches to remain open for a few days, then fill them with sweet soil. The contaminated soil must on no account be allowed to touch the turf, but must be carefully removed, mixed with quicklime, and allowed to stand in a heap for a few months, turning it over as frequently as possible. The action of the lime and air will sweeten the soil. After this treatment it may be used on the borders of the garden, but not on the turf, for fear of accidents.

Sheep, under certain conditions, will manure the grass, keep it short, and, by constantly moving about, help to give the turf a firm surface, and this assists in saving expense of cutting, rolling, and manuring. They can be grazed with advantage in the spring and early summer, provided they are cake or artificially fed. Breeding ewes are seldom given much cake or roots till they have lambed. If not cake or artifically fed, sheep do little good other than keeping the grass short. Even on old pastures they are apt to pull out the small grass rootlets, and for this reason should not be allowed on new grass under any circumstances until it is ascertained that the roots are strong enough to resist being lifted. The droppings from the sheep are always more or less an inconvenience to those playing on a golf green, and in the dry weather scalds are very frequent.

To sum the matter up briefly: if proprietors do not mind the expense of cutting, rolling, and manuring, I see no reason why sheep should be introduced. I have explained the only good they can possibly do under the best circumstances, while, if not cake fed, they may impoverish the land, and in any case are more or less a nuisance on grass that is being played upon, particularly on a putting green. On a garden lawn or similarly confined space their presence would be impossible.

Putting greens should consist of a very fine, dense, and uniform turf, and weeds should not be permitted to exist in them. To get greens into good condition, and keep them up to the mark, is really a work of art, especially when one takes into consideration the varying conditions under which they are expected to flourish. One green may face the north, another the east; one may be on high ground, another on low ground; one is too wet, another too dry; one is on good soil, but most are on poor soil, and all are expected to be in good play practically all the year round.

Consequently, when making a green, do it well: do not stint anything, either in quality or quantity, in labour, manure, or seed, and when a green is in good condition keep it in good condition by continually freeing it from weeds and keeping the turf up to the highest standard, by top-dressing it as frequently as possible, and by constantly repairing weak or bare places with turfs taken from the nursery.

CHAPTER III

TREATMENT AND UPKEEP OF SEASIDE LINKS

By Hugh Hamilton

The subject of the upkeep of greens under present-day requirements has reached a point of the utmost importance, and it is only by the most careful study and attention that a greenkeeper can expect to be successful in his work.

One of the most frequent complaints made by golfers is about the condition of putting greens, the principal cause of which is the greens getting worn out and run down in condition, thereby becoming untrue. The stress of a heavy season's golfing is such that only the most improved methods will keep the turf in the necessary championship form.

The question therefore arises as to the means whereby the greens can be kept up to the same standard in which they were in their virginity and yet sustain the heavy tax to which they are subject at the present day. Should the greens, however, unfortunately become run down, and the mischief is not too pronounced, I strongly advocate nursing the natural turf. Undoubtedly the best means to do so is to rest the greens, but the time during which they would best recover, viz., the spring and autumn, is the height of the golfing season. This course cannot be adopted unless there is a reserve green.

Many are under the erroneous impression that greens recover during the winter months. This is not so: the greens only rest, and do not recover, this not being the time of year when nature is at work to give fresh growth.

As a remedy, the best thing is to make use of the top spits of the natural soil of the links when it can be had; but where the conditions of lease are such that this cannot be got, I advise a mixture of soil and sand, proportioned so as to come as near as possible to the natural soil. This, mixed with a good chemical manure (which is a plant food and not a mere stimulant), has a most beneficial result.

It sometimes happens that, when a green is worn bare after a heavy season, a strong autumn gale blows the bare portions into little cups. When this occurs, the plan is to go over the green and fill all the little holes with the mixture, and stamp it firmly in; then spread it evenly over the green, and brush it well in with a soft, birch broom. When the greens are very bad, this treatment has to be repeated during the winter and spring months, or until there is again a true putting surface.

Farmyard manure is advocated by many as

a food for the greens, but I have strong objections to the use of this. My principal objection is that farmyard manure introduces many of the abominable weeds foreign to the seaside course, by the undigested seeds contained in the droppings of farm animals. One of the worst of these is the plantain, a weed which is well known to be always found in pasture land. Even though farmyard manure were free from those objections, it could not be used if the greens were to be kept in daily use. This difficulty is entirely obviated by the use of a suitable artificial manure. Should the green, however, be utterly run down and past nursing, the only satisfactory method is returfing. This often proves a failure if done with old turf, as, after it is transplanted, it proves of such a leathery nature that it will not take in water. The water simply runs over its surface, and reaches the soil at the joints where the grass is always to be found green, while the centre patch of each turf is often dead. An excellent plan for Green Committees would be to establish nurseries for the growth of turf, which should be transplanted when about three years old, this being an age when the turf would stand wear, and take more kindly to transplanting.

In returfing seaside courses it is essential, when preparing the ground, that good loamy soil should be thoroughly mixed with the sandy soil of the links so as to ensure a growth. It is quite useless to lay turf on pure sand, and equally as

STEPS IN BUNKER (TO SAVE SAND BLOWING).

THE "MAIDEN" (A FINE "FEATURE" BUT NOT A GOOD HAZARD).

bad to put a layer of soil on the top of sand, as it only cakes. Avoid in this case also the use of farmyard manure, both for the reason already stated and because it causes too strong a growth.

Provided that the returfing has been a success, it takes several years before the sward reaches its original fine texture, so that returfing should be a last resort after nursing up the old turf has failed.

Mowing.

Having got the greens into condition, mowing is a very simple matter, especially where the several grasses of the green are of the same nature of growth, as on the greens on Portmarnock Golf Course, Co. Dublin, and on the second, fifth, thirteenth, fifteenth, and home green at St. Andrews; but unfortunately in too many cases when the greens were requiring patching they were patched in the winter months with the turf, which looked beautiful and green, without taking into consideration that grasses foreign to the soil were introduced. This turf, which looked so nice and green during the winter, was introduced to many courses through a common practice some years back, of sowing ordinary hay seed in places where turf had been lifted, whereas it is a well-known fact that all the finer festuca varieties lie dormant during the winter months, looking white and sickly. The result of this process is the introduction of undesirable grass to the greens, making mowing difficult, as perennial rye grass and nearly all varieties contained in permanent pasture rush into growth much quicker than the natural grasses indigenous to the soil. Therefore, to keep a true putting surface, instead of mowing once in about ten days during dry weather, where those grasses have been introduced mowing must be resorted to every other day to keep the surface true and level.

This too frequent mowing gives punishment to the greens which might under other circumstances have been avoided; but of the two evils mowing is the lesser, as everyone knows that perennial ryegrass sends up a strong seed-stalk—an obstruction which no golfer cares to meet with in the line of his putt. At the same time, no definite rule can be set down in regard to mowing: the local circumstances must guide each greenkeeper, but the less mowing in dry weather the better for the greens. Another grievous evil which the introduction of these seeds brings about is that after the greens have been top-dressed the strong grasses spring into growth, and during a dry gale of wind part of the dressing is blown about, and finds a resting-place against the tufts formed by the rye-grass, thus making miniature mounds.

Rolling.

In regard to rolling, where the sward is good, rolling is not very necessary during the winter months. I have never found regular rolling do any harm during the growing season, say, from April to September, but where the sward is in the condition mentioned in the last paragraph, rolling becomes a necessity during the winter months, and this is a period when one must be careful, more especially during very wet or frosty weather. Greens should never be rolled until the frost is thoroughly out of the ground, and during wet weather it is also detrimental to roll, as it cakes the surface too much, and the rain, during the summer months, does not sink equally into the ground, but runs off the higher parts into the hollows, leaving the green very patchy-looking. Therefore, the greenkeeper would do better to listen to a few complaints than spoil the green by over-rolling during the winter months.

Worms.

On seaside courses in my experience there is not much trouble on account of worms. At St. Andrews very few are found further out than the third hole. Where they are too plentiful, as at the Home Green, St. Andrews, by all means get rid of them. They were removed from this green early in the spring of 1905, and the green during the summer was ever so much keener and truer than formerly. Where the worms are plentiful in the neighbourhood of a green they soon reassert themselves.

I cannot help thinking that where worms are

they form a natural seed bed for daises, etc., for where a patch of daises is found on a green otherwise clear of weeds the ground at that patch contains worms. No seeds can germinate on a close sward of turf, but the worm makes a little hole all ready to receive any seeds that may be blown about or dropped by animals, etc. Portmarnock course is an instance proving that turf can thrive without worms, as the greens there are perfect and almost entirely free of weeds.

Weeds.

There are many good lawn sands on the market which will kill daisies without injury to the turf, but such weeds as the common plantain, dandelion, plantago, or star weed, can only be got rid of by " howking " them out.

Seeding.

Now for a word regarding seeds, the sowing of which on all much frequented golf courses has become a necessity. Due care should be taken to see that iron cuts and bare patches, as well as areas showing a thin tendency, be repaired without loss of time, otherwise the expense of such repairs will be all the heavier later on.

Certain grasses may grow on almost any soil, but a preference is generally shown, and, while attention must be directed to those varieties specially which have a dwarf, close habit of growth, this preference for soil and situation must be carefully noted in making selections. Among the many grasses and plants that constitute, generally, the turf on our East Coast seaside links, which the observant greenkeeper will, no doubt, have noticed for himself, are the various fescues and poas, the crested dogstail, vernals, and rent grasses (*Nardus molinia*, etc.), together with yarrow, wild thyme, and small-leaved clovers, of various kinds, while here and there, in damp places, the *Carex* sedge and heath rush will be found. Rye-grass may unfortunately be present, but should never be introduced into any mixture of seeds for the best seaside courses. Where putting greens are sown down, I think the fewer varieties used the better, and these varieties ought to be of the same nature of growth, otherwise the green will have a tufty appearance. Many may think it ridiculous on my part to advocate introducing to putting greens such a variety as *Agrostis vulgaris*, judging from its appearance in a natural wild state, but I know of no better wearing variety.

On seaside courses, my impression is that nothing more is required than a mixture composed of the following varieties :—Hard fescue (*Festuca duriuscula*), red fescue (*Festuca ovina*), fine-leaved sheep's fescue (*Festuca ovina tenuifolia*), yarrow (*Achillea*), with about twenty per cent. of *Agrostis vulgaris millifolium*). My reason for advocating this variety of *Agrostis vulgaris*, which is not found in any putting green mixture on the market, is on account of my experience of its unerring and true putting qualities at St. Andrews, where it is to be found on the east side of the fifth and thirteenth greens and on the north side of the ninth green. The hole in these parts will stand good for a week in the height of the season, while in some of the other greens the hole has to be shifted daily. All golfers playing over the greens mentioned will find the putting conditions perfect.

Teeing Grounds.

I, along with others, have gone on a wrong basis in laying teeing grounds with ordinary turf, as experience clearly shows that this will not stand present-day requirements. Instead of using fine turf, such as is found through the greens, I have discovered that the best teeing grounds are obtained by turfing (when procurable) with the mat grass (*Nardus stricta*) and *Agrostis vulgaris*, two varieties which are nearly always found growing together, and are almost indestructible. This can be seen at St. Andrews, where these species are to be found on the winter tee going to the fifth hole, at the approach shot to the thirteenth (on the right), at the approach to the ninth and tenth, and on the right of the approach going to the fourth hole. When the teeing ground has to be laid on low-lying or damp ground, the best thing to use is a mixture of the mat grass (*Nardus stricta*) and the heath

IN THE MARRAM (LYME GRASS).

LYME GRASS—STOPPING SAND BLOWING.

rush (*Juncus squarrosus*). Some golfers might object to this variety, as it is so hard that a sclafed tee shot would not go off so well as off the ordinary soft turf.

Through the Greens.

Where returfing is required at the approach shot, all the varieties already mentioned for teeing grounds ought to be used instead of the ordinary fine turf. For iron cuts, the best remedy is soil and sand mixed as near the nature of natural soil as possible, with a touch of seed thrown in. The best time to fill the cuts is early in April and again in August. The seed is all the better to be mixed with the soil until it shows signs of germinating before applying. The three varieties mentioned as indestructible are not contained, however, so far as I am aware, in any mixture on the market. It is important that seeds for iron cuts and bare parts should be of the same varieties as those found on the links, and the greenkeeper will be wise to take his seeds only from the expert seedsman who has made golf grasses and links plants a study and who can supply mixtures of seeds. The value of their knowledge and of their mixtures is shown in the remarkable results of the so-called "Strongholds," which will, with almost perfect accuracy, reproduce the existing turf of any golf course, no matter what its situation, proportioning the grasses out in their different percentages and giving due prominence to the predominating grasses, while not forgetting those other humbler but no less useful heath plants which combine to form that smooth sward suitable for the demands of the up-to-date golf course.

Blown Sand.

Referring to blown sand from the beach, banking with railway sleepers, or any other manner of solid banking, only adds to the evil, etc. This manner of banking simply acts as a natural shoot whereby the sand, when blown by a strong gale, rises higher, and is distributed over a larger area. In fact, on seaside courses where this manner of banking is adopted the sand, during a high wind, is raised as by a natural gully fifty to a hundred feet in the air. Where such sandstorms occur, the best way to obviate the evil is to place a double fence of $\frac{1}{2}$-inch wire netting, tacked to posts, six inches separating the lines of netting. Where it has been tried, this method has shown the most satisfactory results. The wind and sand moving in a solid body, the open netting breaks up the force, and the sand, being the heavier body, drops behind the obstruction. St. Andrews is a capital illustration of how the lyme grass can fight sand and sea. The introduction of this grass has conferred the greatest benefit, as is shown by the land reclaimed from the sea on a line from the old sand dune at the rifle target, where several hundred acres have been reclaimed.

It is quite interesting to notice how the lyme grass spreads itself seawards, gradually forming little sand dunes stretching in a line below high water mark. These little sand dunes soon unite, and form a natural embankment. About fifty yards behind this line follow the bents, and behind that again follows the hard sheep's fescue. The lyme grass has proved most efficient at St. Andrews in the preventing of blown sand from the beach, and it could be adopted with equal benefit on other seaside courses. Especially does this apply to North Berwick, from Hutchison's shop to Pointgarry, and between the Pit hole and Eelburn. The lyme grass is a wonderful reclaimer, and always stretches seawards.

Summing Up.

To sum up in regard to the keeping of putting greens, this can only be done satisfactorily by having a plentiful supply of water, a commodity which I have never yet found in sufficiency on any seaside course. The water obtainable is usually contained in sunken wells, and lacks the essential qualities found in running water. Moreover, the water in those wells very often contains a mineral—iron, etc.—and, when put on the green, forms a crust through which the rain does not penetrate, the water running off the higher parts into the hollows. This, of course, I admit, would not be the case if the water were sufficient, and the quantity stored were adequate. As a remedy, I would propose laying a 3-inch pipe right through every seaside course, with a hydrant and sprinkler at every green. If this were adopted the greenkeeper could be quite happy during a dry season, instead of, as under the present condition, seeing his greens worn out day after day, and himself helplessly looking on. If there was a sufficient supply of water, very little seeding, manuring, or returfing would be required. This is the only measure, in my opinion, by which the greens can be kept up to the mark.

It is worth quoting, on this point, an American's opinion, with whom I recently had a conversation on the subject. He said, "If we had a links like you have at St. Andrews, I guess we should keep the greens properly watered, if it took a pipe made of gold to convey the water out to the end hole."

CHAPTER IV

TYPICAL ENGLISH EAST COAST LINKS.—DEAL

By HENRY HUNTER

IN accordance with request, I have jotted down a few remarks on greenkeeping, particularly as to my practice on the links of the Cinque Ports Golf Club, Deal, where I have been professional and greenkeeper for the past fourteen years.

Mowing.

There is not very much I can say under this head, except that I prefer to have the box on the mowing machine when on the putting green, the use of the box being to prevent the spreading of weeds, and that I have found a 10-inch machine the most handy to use. I prefer Green's to any other make. Neither the course nor the greens should be cut too close in the early spring, or when there is a north-east wind, as this wind dries us up quicker even than a hot sun.

Rolling.

I am not in favour of too much rolling when once the ground is properly set, but occasional rolling and dragging with a chain harrow in the winter do good in removing rubbish out of the grass and letting in light and air to the roots. I always use wooden rollers on the greens, and believe them to be better than iron ones.

Seeding.

After many trials of various grass seeds, I have found Sutton's special mixture for golf links to give the best results. The seed should be sown during the latter part of August, so as to catch the late summer rains. Seed sown at this time is well established before the winter.

Worming.

I cannot say very much about this as we are never troubled with too many worms on this light, sandy soil, but whenever I see there are too many, I reduce the numbers. I do not believe in trying to get rid of them altogether.

Manuring.

Both for the course and greens there is nothing to equal good stable manure, well rotted down, and used as fine as possible. This, after being spread, should be continually moved about with a chain-drag. I spread the manure as early in February as possible. Besides other advantages, the use of this manure enables the links to have a much-needed rest—few golfers caring to play while the links are covered.

Watering.

This is absolutely necessary in dry weather, to keep the grass alive. The watering is best done at night, though in dull weather not much harm will be caused if done in the daytime.

Planting of Marram Grass.

This grass is extremely useful in preventing sand from blowing. We entirely stopped the sand from blowing out of "Sandy Parlour" by planting this grass. We did not raise it from seed, but transplanted from another part of the links. The best time for planting in this way is the end of February.

In the making and building up of the sides of bunkers, I have found the system of revetting to be the best. There is one very important item in greenkeeping, and that is weeding. This should be done in the spring, when the sap is rising in the weeds, because, if you are not fortunate enough to get out the whole of the root, the breaking of it will probably cause the plant to bleed to death. Our greatest pest in the way of weeds is the "star," or, as it is generally known, the "Brancaster weed." I have never found any preparation or poison to give permanent results, and believe the only way to deal with weeds is to keep them under by constantly weeding with a *three*-pronged fork.

CHAPTER V

TREATMENT AND UPKEEP OF A GOLF COURSE ON LIGHT INLAND SOIL

By H. S. COLT

BEFORE commencing to make a golf course no effort should be spared to obtain a thoroughly sound tenancy of the land. It is most desirable, if possible, to purchase the freehold, but if this be out of the question, then a lease of the land—not merely of the golfing rights over the land—should be obtained for as long a term as possible. A lease for twenty-one years is not long enough, as large sums of money will have to be spent on constructing the course, and if this expense has to be written off in the accounts of the club in twenty-one years, it will prove too heavy a strain on the finances. Moreover, the club will not reap a sufficient benefit from this capital expenditure. In a number of cases the land, when first acquired, has little value for agricultural purposes, but at the end of the term of the lease it will probably be improved, and for this improvement the club will then obtain no return: on the contrary, it will, as often as not, be told to go elsewhere, or made to pay a heavily increased rent. It is often argued that the landlord is sure to deal favourably with the club on the termination of the lease, as his other land in the neighbourhood of the course will be much improved by its close proximity to the links. But many things may occur in the interval, and no club should be placed in such a position that the landlord is able to dictate his terms. The fact remains that, unless the freehold of the land be bought, or a lease for forty-two years at least be obtained, the club will have a bad bargain. If a good margin of the course can also be obtained, so much the better, as this land will be almost certain to possess considerable building value in the future. Golfing rights alone are most unsatisfactory, as the tenant farmer's grazing rights will have to be dealt with, otherwise horses and cattle may destroy the greens and be an intolerable nuisance.

Proximity to a railway station will, no doubt, be sought for, and if it can be obtained, will add greatly to the success of the undertaking.

Before laying out the course, a large scale Ordnance map should be purchased, and a thorough knowledge of the lie of land obtained by every possible means. To get this knowledge it will be necessary to constantly walk over the land, to try shots, and to gain local information.

In the meantime an analysis should be made of the soil, or, at anyrate, the amount of carbonate of lime present in it should be ascertained. Samples of the soil, or turves cut from the land if it is already in turf, should be sent to a first-class seed merchant, and one in whom perfect reliance can be placed. If there is no turf, it may prove a help to the seed merchant to send turves from adjoining properties if the soil is similar in character. Impress upon him the necessity of having, if possible, grasses similar to the indigenous grasses, provided they are suitable for golf. The term "if possible" is used advisedly, as they may not be on the market, owing to their lack of nutritive value for cattle. The first portion to be sown should be a piece of ground for a turf nursery. This will prove to be of great help afterwards. An acre or two of good sound turf, free from weeds, is always one of the club's best assets, and in the case of a new course is almost invaluable for repairs or new greens. On soils of a light sandy nature, a grass known by the name of *Agrostis vulgaris* may be included in the mixture. Messrs. Sutton, the well-known seed merchants of Reading, can supply this, and, if carefully cut, this grass, although not usually included in mixtures, affords good putting. It will be best to have a mixture of grasses and not depend on one sort alone.

The sites of the putting greens will be determined, to a great extent, by the natural features of the course. But in the selection of these sites

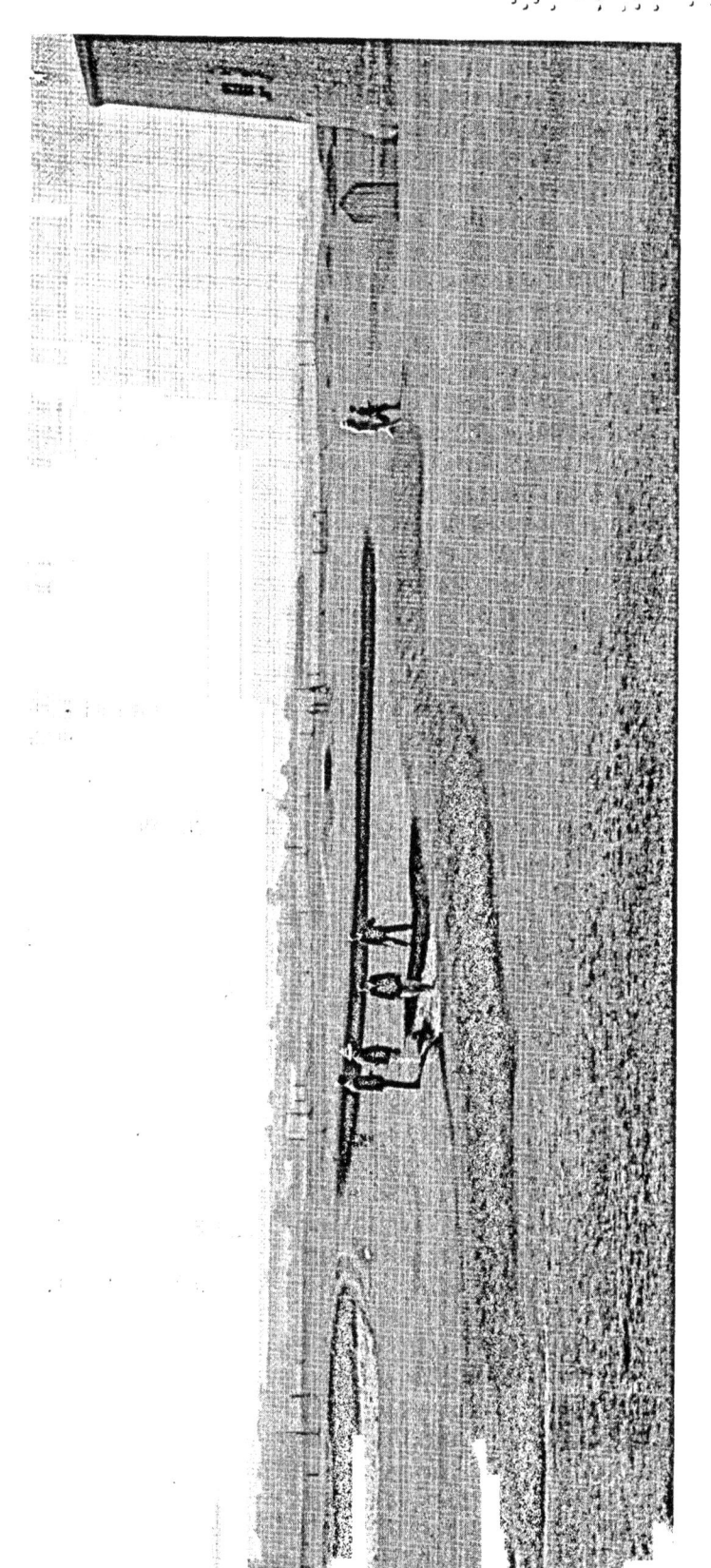

FELIXSTOWE LINKS.

WATER HAZARD—INLAND COURSE.

blind shots should be avoided wherever possible. This more especially applies to blind approach shots and to blind short holes. Probably one of the greatest pleasures in golf is to watch a well struck approach shot receive satisfactory treatment on its pitch. A preponderance of good two-shot holes of about 400 yards are, of course, desirable, and will be arranged for if possible.

In this class of hole a compulsory carry for second shots should surely be avoided. Under certain conditions of wind, the hazards will, of a necessity, become impossible. The cross hazard for the second shot will not be absolutely safe for the exceptionally long driver from the tee under 260 yards or so, and, if placed there, the shorter driver will not be able to attempt to carry it in his second shot when playing against any wind but a light breeze. Therefore, it is now urged that the compulsory carry for the second shot be dropped altogether. This does not advocate that there should be no hazards for second shots, but only that a route round them should be provided. If the hazard for the second shot can be put in such a position that the player is forced to place his tee shot in order to have a clear line to the hole for his second shot, so much the better. It is this "placing" of the tee shot which is so difficult to most players, and this should be borne in mind during the construction of the course. In laying out the holes, first-class golf must, no doubt, be the primary consideration, but if you value the peace of mind of the Green Committee, have a regard for the long handicap player.

A long hole, with a bend or twist in it, or possibly a double swing like an elongated S, is a good type of hole. As an instance of this, the seventeenth hole on the old course at St. Andrews may be mentioned. It was especially good in the old days of the gutty ball. A player who had a good score up to that point in his medal round, at the autumn meeting of the club, and played it correctly and registered a five, must have felt more than satisfied. Personally, this has never been my lot, as an average of ten for this hole was my fate during a series of years. The above hole also provides an example of the great value of bunkers cut close up to the holes. A bunker stretching right across the course should always be avoided, and, unless there are natural hazards, "pot" bunkers are preferable to others.

In selecting a site for a putting green, if there is a choice of one facing due south or due north, use discretion in the selection. For example, on the south coast of England a green facing due south is liable to be burnt up in hot weather, and, no doubt, in bleak, cold spots, grass in greens facing north may be slow in making a start in the early spring.

Now that the sites of the greens have been selected, if there is turf, use it if possible. It is astonishing how quickly the rough, natural turf improves with good treatment. It must first be thoroughly weeded, and the only satisfactory way to do this is to stretch two lines across the green, three or four yards apart, and thus weed it in sections with weeding forks, as the patent weed-killing implements are dangerous to the surrounding grass. Having done this, if the turf is poor, rake the surface with sharp rakes which will cut the turf. Strong rakes should be obtained, and the teeth filed sharp. Do not be afraid of tearing or cutting up the turf, because this is the only way whereby a good bed for seed can be obtained. A rich, light dressing of soil and stable manure, taken from stables where horses are highly fed, should now be applied. It will be better not to use chemical manures at this time, and it will be an advantage to pass the dressing through a $\frac{1}{2}$-inch or 1-inch screen. The seed can then be sown and raked into the soil, and rolled down firm if it is not too wet.

If there is no turf suitable for renovation on the sites of the greens, then the land must be ploughed up as deeply as possible, or, better still, trenched. If drainage is necessary, this must now be done, and special care must be taken to properly drain under the bank in the case of greens cut out from a slope. In draining putting greens it is a good plan to keep the drains nearer the surface than usually is done, and to use a 6-inch or 4-inch main, with 2-inch branch drains in the form of a herring bone. Care should always be taken not to put the branch drains at right angles to the main drains, as the water flowing in by the branch drains will obviously tend to obstruct the water flowing down the upper portion of the main drain. Obtain as good a fall as is possible, and never drain straight down a slope, but always diagonally across it.

The land should now be well dressed with chalk or lime, if the soil analysis shows that this is wanting. If lime is used, there should be an interval before a good dressing of manure is applied. This is necessary owing to the fact that, if the manure and lime were applied together, the latter would free a considerable percentage of the ammonia present in the manure, which would thus be wasted in the atmosphere. Fork in the dressing of chalk or lime and the manure, and then choose between seed or local turf taken from a similar soil. If turf were taken from a heavy clay soil and laid upon a light, sandy one, the chances are that it would not prove satisfactory. If seed be used, the land must be thoroughly worked so that there is a fine tilth, and it will be difficult to obtain this unless the weather be dry. Perhaps the soil is exceedingly poor, and in this case it will prove a great help to give a coating of rich soil, some three inches in depth, over the site for the proposed greens.

Grass seed may be sown in the spring or

the autumn, but there is a great difference of opinion as to which is the better time. It is suggested here that probably the early autumn (about the beginning of September) is the best time in the south of England, as in this district drought is certainly more to be feared for young grass than hard frost; whereas, in the North, possibly the reverse might apply. But young grass plants seem to stand frost better than drought, and if a long spell of dry weather follows the sowing of the seed, the plants are sure to come up "patchy."

The seed may be sown either by hand or by a seed-drill. Generally in the neighbourhood there is a man who excels at this work, and whose services can be engaged. A still day is necessary, as some grass seeds are very light, It is better to go over the ground twice than to use up all the seed in one sowing. Six to eight bushels of seed to the acre is ample, although some recommend as much as twelve bushels.

The natural undulations of the ground will no doubt be retained, and possibly some artificial ones will be created. Perfectly flat putting is uninteresting, but greens of a very undulating nature are not easy to keep in good order, as the grass growing on the banks is more difficult to feed, and, of course, such greens afford fewer positions for the holes, and ought, therefore, to be proportionately larger. Any sharp banks or hills will need to be modified, otherwise there will be some impossible putts.

Now, to proceed with the construction of the course through the green. If turf exists, let this be thoroughly rolled and drained where necessary. If the grass be poor, a good dressing of light soil and manure will be needed, and the soil analysis will show what is wanted. Probably stable manure, with some chemical manures added to it, will be best, but each individual case will need careful consideration. The more experience that anyone has in greenkeeping the less likely is he to make any definite and general statement on the subject of chemical manures. A member of a club may very often be heard to lay down the law, in no uncertain terms, that basic slag, or some other artificial or chemical manure, must be used, as it proved a success elsewhere—the soil and conditions being quite different. By all means try different manures if previous treatment has not been successful, but at first only do this by way of experiment. If, however, the soil lacks carbonate of lime, it is almost useless to apply manures until this deficiency has been supplied by the addition of chalk or lime. In the case of some turf it may be advisable to use heavy iron drag harrows on the surface and then follow up with a dressing without chemical manures, and sow seed and roll firm.

If no turf be present, and the unfortunate greenkeeper is provided with a prairie, desert, or sour heath land, and expected to produce, without delay, perfect lies over a course perhaps containing well over a hundred acres, then his lot will be an unhappy one for two or three years. He must be prepared to hear criticism from every member of the club, to have his methods discussed and probably condemned in every corner of the smoking-room of the club-house, to be confronted with the opinions of members' gardeners—no doubt worthy men and excellent growers of tomatoes and cucumbers, but possibly without any previous experience in greenkeeping. For a certainty he will have to contend with the opinions of members of the Green Committees of other clubs which have existed for years, and probably started their course on fine, old, common turf or down land. He will be told that it is extraordinary what treatment grass will stand if success begins to dawn upon his miserable efforts. And all this because the golfer thinks that any silly fool can grow grass. But this will not matter much so long as he retains the confidence of his Green Committee and is allowed to persevere.

To make a start on heather land with a light soil and probably some peat present in it, the first step will be to plough up the land as deep as possible, using a sub-soil plough in addition to the ordinary type. It is a great advantage to get a deep tilth and also to break through the "pan" or strong crust underneath the surface which is prevalent in this class of land. Then collect the heather and rough grasses by means of drag harrows and burn them slowly. If they are burnt in a quick fire the ash will not be so valuable as a manure. Harrow the surface until a fine tilth is obtained, and then add carbonate of lime in some form if the analysis shows a deficiency, and this will very likely be the case on this class of soil. Distribute the ashes from the fires over the land, and afterwards apply the manure needed, and harrow or plough it in lightly. What has been said about the construction of putting greens when seed is sown will obviously apply to the present work, with these exceptions, that the luxury of some additional soil will not be possible over a large area, and four to six bushels of seed per acre will be sufficient. The dressing of stable manure before the seed is sown should be at the rate of about twenty tons to the acre. As to the mixture of seed, use the mixture previously used for the nurseries, comprised, if possible, of suitable indigenous grasses, and on the class of course now being considered, add some white dwarf creeping clover, *Trifolium repens.* This would not be advisable for putting greens, but through the green it helps wonderfully to fill up the gaps as it creeps along the surface, and, when cut, provides good lies. It is a perennial clover, and if helped from time to time with a suitable manure, such as basic slag, it will flourish, but not to the detriment of the grass. The clover will, to a certain extent, assist the grass, as it will, by its roots, or—if the technical term may be used—by its "nodules," which are like small bulbs attached to the roots, store up nitrogen from the atmosphere for the use of the grass plants. This may be proved by examining a clover patch in dry weather. The surrounding grass may look dry and in poor condition, but if the clover patch is examined carefully, grasses will be found growing freely among the clover plants. I am not advocating the indiscriminate use of clovers of any kind on all soils, but only the use of the white perennial creeping clover on a light sandy soil with a percentage of peat present in it, and it would probably be safe to use this clover on any light soil.

Before dealing with the general upkeep of the greens of the course, it may be as well now to refer to the construction of the artificial hazards. It is, no doubt, the best plan to make as few as possible until the links have been played over for at least six months. Then nick out the proposed sites and play for a further three months. By this time the course will have been thoroughly tested under all conditions, and although it may get faster when the turf consolidates, and the ball thus gain a trifle more run, still, this can then be taken into account and the hazards cut.

Very large bunkers mean increased cost in upkeep, and very deep ones will probably give rise to difficult drainage: so let these points receive some consideration. If possible, use turf on heath land, or turves cut from the heather, for the sides of the bunkers, and not the refuse from the nearest railway station in the shape of old sleepers. If the face of a bunker needs raising it is advisable to avoid placing a grass bank or mound on the top, but in its place insert or slip, so to speak, soil between the turf and existing soil. Of course the turf will have to be first removed and afterwards replaced upon the added soil, which will be sloped in a low gradient to the surrounding ground. The face of the hazard will then appear more natural—in fact, as if it had been cut out of a mound.

The construction of the greens has been discussed, but nothing has been said as to their size. This must always largely depend upon the circumstances of each individual case, such as the lie of the land, the probable amount of play, the funds at the disposal of the club for the upkeep of the course, and, doubtless, many other matters. From a greenkeeper's point of view, it is better to have greens wide and shallow than narrow and deep. In the first case, if a portion needs repair, or resting, he can easily move the hole from one side to the other, but if a deep and narrow green needs attention in the portion nearest to the tee, he is unable to rope it off without closing the whole green, and golf links, unlike cricket or football or lawn tennis grounds, are required for play during the whole of the year. The greenkeeper has no quiet three months for the repair of the course. Therefore, if much play is anticipated, let the greens be wide enough—say, forty yards—or let there be a subsidiary green at each hole, which can be used in rough weather, such as a thaw following a hard frost, as well as during the repair of the regular green.

On new greens the first object should be to promote a healthy, strong growth of grass, and it is only by having this that a good putting surface can be obtained. How often on new courses the excessive use of the heavy roller has flattened out a more or less smooth surface at the expense of a healthy growth of grass! A first-class green has never been made by the heavy roller. Frequent rolling with light rollers, three feet or so in width, and weighing a hundredweight to a hundredweight and a half, is undoubtedly beneficial, and a turn with the heavy roller occasionally is a great help, but the excessive use of the heavy roller used to be one of the commonest faults in greenkeeping. The effect of too much rolling is to cake the surface of the green. The atmosphere then cannot reach the roots of the grass, and, if this takes place, they will die for a certainty. A thoroughly porous soil must be obtained and retained.

Bush-harrowing is an excellent thing, and proves a great help, and sharp sea-sand and charcoal aid in retaining this porousness. But if a green becomes badly caked, one of the best things to do is to ease the surface of the whole green with forks, and give a dressing of sharp sea-sand, which will work into the holes made by the forks. The surface being porous, in the case of new greens now proceed to feed the grass and promote a strong growth. The question of manures is too large a subject to discuss thoroughly in this chapter, and I am not competent enough to attempt to write in detail upon it. But there are two elementary points in agricultural chemistry which must always be borne in mind when feeding grass. The first is that carbonate of lime must be present in the soil, and therefore, if lacking, it must be added. The second is that the three main plant foods consist of nitrates, phosphates, and potash, and in feeding grass, nitrate is specially needed, but the others must also be present. A dressing of rich light garden loam is very effective. Liquid manure made from dung and pumped over the green from tubs on the spot is a great help in the early stages of a green. Take care, however, that it is well diluted with water, otherwise it will scorch the grass. A good dressing of well-decayed stable manure is undoubtedly good for a green at this stage, but, possibly, Peruvian guano is better, as there is no risk of weeds being brought in the manure. Poultry manure, if used with caution, is excellent, and much richer than stable manure. All these would act as good general manures, and the loam and dung would contain a large percentage of humus or decayed vegetable matter which may be necessary to prevent a green on a light sandy soil from drying out in its early stages. The soil analysis will help in the selection of the most suitable form of manure. The primary object must be to obtain by plentiful feeding a good coat of grass over the whole of the green. This can be fined down in the subsequent stages. Having once obtained this, and retained the porous surface, more than half the battle is over; and on some soils it is a battle!

It may now be as well soon to drop the use of such organic manures as stable manure and rich loam, as, if used too freely, they are likely to encourage worms. A green, rich in humus, is almost certainly rich in worms, and every greenkeeper knows what a nuisance they are. So let the green be only sufficiently rich in humus to prevent it from drying out too quickly in drought, otherwise there will be a plague of worms. No doubt they may do good on ordinary pasture land, but they are an abomination to the golfer, especially on the putting green. There are, however, many effective worm-killers in the market, and these should be used freely. Charcoal is said to act as a preventive on some soils, and lime water is an old and well-known remedy.

The green must now be kept growing in a healthy state, and light dressings of guano or some inorganic manure will effect this. If proprietary manures are used, be careful to get good value. After reading the analyses and evaluation made by the well-known expert, Mr. A. D. Hall, the greenkeeper will become somewhat sceptical about the advantages claimed for these manures. The dressings may be applied in the early spring and early autumn, and, if possible, this should be done in showery weather, as if a spell of hot weather ensues the grass may become scorched. These dressings are always rather anxious work owing to this, and if there is water laid on for use at the greens it will be best to use it freely on the evening following the application if the weather is likely to be hot or dry. Play on the course need not be interfered with to any great extent if the heaps of dressing are placed at each green ready for use, and the work is done in the following manner :—On inland courses the busy days for play are almost invariably Saturdays and Sundays. Therefore let all the heaps be ready on the Saturday, and first thing on Monday morning crowd on all hands to this work, brush the dressing in carefully with *new* birch brooms, and the next day sweep off what is left. Thus, by the following Wednesday or Thursday there will be practically no inconvenience, and the grass will have received sufficient encouragement to start off once again in its struggle with the heavy-booted player. The banks of a green will very often need more of the dressing than the hollows, and it is not a bad plan to pierce the surface of the banks with the prongs of a fork and work the dressing carefully into the holes. After a dressing always use old mowing machines, as, however carefully the work has been done, there will always be a few undesirable relics left lurking about in search of the knives of your best new machine.

Nothing, so far, has been said as to cutting the grass. For the first cutting after sowing seed it is probably best to use sharp scythes, but good mowing machines have been known to do the work well. The grass must not be allowed to get too long for a mowing machine at any period, but when the grass has become established a machine must, of course, be used, and for the finest work good roller machines will be found the best. Unless the greens are flat the machines had better not be more than sixteen inches in width, otherwise the hollows will be difficult to cut. The outsides of the greens may be cut with the American type of machine, with side wheels, as this will save labour. The blades and cutting plates must be carefully looked after and kept sharp, and the former must be properly set, otherwise the grass will be cut in ridges. The head greenkeeper must attend to this carefully. Keep, if possible, a new machine always in readiness for a big match day. The men should not always cut a green in the same direction, but, on the contrary, they should take a different "route" every time, including in their turns diagonal cutting. Whenever there is any grass to cut, then cut it as close to the surface as possible without injuring the crowns of the plants. There is, no doubt, a difference of opinion about this, and some greenkeepers raise the knives of the machines in summer with a view to affording protection to the plants during a drought. This may be a good plan with young grass laid on a green facing south or west in a very hot district, but the pleasure of golf vanishes when attempting to putt on such a green, resembling a thick pile carpet more than anything else. On established turf, close cutting will do no harm, especially if the roots of the grass have plenty to feed on. And if there is a healthy growth of grass before the drought sets in, the roots of the grass are not likely to be in the least degree damaged by a long spell of dry weather.

The cutting plates of machines vary considerably, and for the finest work a machine with a thin plate appears to be the best—in fact, the thinner the better. But such a machine can only be used on a green absolutely free from stones, as they would obviously damage a thin plate much more than a thick one. In my opinion, there is one machine on the market which is in advance of all others which have been tried, and they have been numerous, and if any reader should think it worth while to write and ask its name I shall be very

GENERAL ASPECT OF SANDWICH.

TO THE ELEVENTH HOLE, WESTWARD HO!

pleased to give it. Before we leave this subject, one word of warning may not be out of place. Never purchase a second-hand mowing machine if you can help it. Sometimes you cannot! They are generally worthless, and although the owners of these articles seem to possess in a very marked degree the power of selling them to their friends, resist the temptation of buying a bargain and save the club scrap-heap from being increased at a very early date.

The pace of the putting green can be increased by the use of sand, and probably sharp sea-sand is the best. It should be the aim of anyone in charge of an inland green to obtain putting of a similar character as far as possible to that afforded by good seaside turf. Every golfer will appreciate the difference between a putting "lawn" and a putting "green," which Mr. Ryder Richardson, the well-known secretary of the Royal St. George's Golf Club, many years ago pointed out to me. And, although it is advocated here that in the early stages of a new green the first endeavour should be to obtain a strong, healthy growth of grass, if the matter was left there, the result would be a putting "lawn": hence the necessity for making the grass finer by the use of sea-sand, which, combined with constant close cutting of the grass, makes it possible, even on inland courses, to obtain fast putting greens (not lawns). The inland golfer will, perhaps, complain that the greens are too fast, but a keen green will test the skill of the player to a far greater extent than a slow lawn. Perhaps greens may become too fast: and many complained that this was the case at a recent Championship. But this is not likely to happen upon inland golf courses if the grass is kept in a healthy state, although some greens will need sea-sand to a far greater extent than others. The expense and difficulty of obtaining it is generally too great for the use of it to be abused.

If the putting greens on a course be carefully examined, anyone can observe that the turf varies considerably in character. Each green will be found to possess an individuality of its own. The growth on one will be strong and inclined to be coarse; on another, clovers will always be present; on another, there will be a tendency for the grass to be poor; and on another the soil may be a trifle sour, and the turf in wet, cold weather will look unhealthy and very likely begin to turn yellow. Each green must in fact be studied by itself, and the treatment modified so that the individual wants of each may as far as possible be supplied. This may all seem to be absurd to the casual player, but let him carefully examine the greens when he is next on a golf course, and he will probably agree. Take, for instance, the old course at St. Andrews: the green at the first hole used to be totally different from that at the High Hole. The varieties of grass growing on two greens of a course are very often quite distinct. A mixture of seed was recently sown in a nursery at Sunningdale, consisting of smooth-stalked meadow grass, fescues in variety, and crested dogstail. There was a ridge in the land, which was, of course, drier than the surrounding ground. On this ridge the turf was quite different from the rest, the fescues were growing strongly and were very largely in preponderance, whereas, in the rest of the nursery, the grasses were growing more equally. This will show how difficult it is to obtain similar turf on all the greens and to prevent variation in the pace. A moderate variety in the putting is, no doubt, an additional test for the player, but this is never likely to be absent, and it is objectionable to come off an exceptionally fast, keen green and find the next hole cut in a feather bed. Therefore, each green should be studied by itself, and treated with a view of obtaining, as far as possible, a uniform standard of putting.

Weeds are sure to come, in spite of every care. The greens should be thoroughly weeded, as previously mentioned, with weeding forks, before the dressings are applied in the spring and autumn. The holes made by taking them out will be filled up by the dressing, and, as the surrounding grass starts into active growth, nothing will be seen of these places unless exceptionally abundant. A little seed used at this time is an additional help. This manner of weeding applies to all such common enemies as dandelions, plantains, and daisies—in fact, to all weeds which do not creep under or along the surface. The latter, of which chick-weed is a type, are more difficult to eradicate, and, unless taken in their very early stage, had better be left alone until the entire sods of turf can be taken out and clean turf from the nursery inserted in their place. The most convenient time to do this work on inland courses will probably be December or January. There is generally less play then than at any other time during the season for laying turf. Any bare patches on the green or tees can also then be repaired, but do not overdo this work by taking out turf which looks a trifle weak, as in many cases, with a rest and some feeding, it will soon come again and do better than fresh turf. For small repairs of this sort a large hole cutter is generally used.

Always cut turf thin; one inch to one and a half inches is quite thick enough. I know that there is a considerable difference of opinion about this, but, from personal experience, I feel convinced that the thinner the turf the better, provided that the crowns of the grass plants are not touched. Such turves start to grow quickly in their new quarters, and possibly the effect of cutting the roots of the plants is to stimulate them to increased action. When the fresh turf has been laid, always put on a light top-dressing and brush it in. This will cause the turves to join up quicker. Before laying the turf make the ground firm by treading or rolling. Newly laid turf should not be used for play until it is rooted.

Old turf is, no doubt, better than young, but it is astonishing how quickly turf will come from seed, especially in a light soil. Seed has, to my knowledge, been sown in September and the grass lifted and laid in the following March for a new green, which was used for play in April and has been used ever since for two or three years, and still affords good putting. It is best to finish all turfing as soon after Christmas as possible. Sometimes the greenkeeper will be forced to lay turf in March or even later, but he runs a great risk in doing so, as a spell of drought or cold east winds may come, and then the turf will be prevented from making a start. The turf, when cut, should be laid quickly and not allowed to lie about in heaps. Frost or cold winds blowing on the freshly cut roots will damage them to a certain extent, and it is best to endeavour to lay in the same day all turf cut during that time.

Moss is generally a sign of bad drainage or poverty. If it is due to poverty, rake it out with sharp rakes, dress the land with lime, and after an interval give some rich light dressing with some soot mixed with it. The term "light dressing" is meant throughout this chapter to imply a dressing of light soil with other manures added. There always appears to be a danger in using heavy or sticky soils for dressings on putting greens, as they cannot be worked into the turf quickly enough, and traffic over grass so dressed is liable to cake the surface. If the moss is due to a want of drainage, this must, of course, be attended to. On some soils moss will come during the winter and disappear altogether in the spring as soon as the grass starts growing again.

Grubs may infest the soil and cause damage to the turf by eating the roots of the grass. I have seen turf almost destroyed by a plague of " leather jackets." Probably a dressing of " Vaporite," if it could be worked into the turf, would prove effective. It is largely used in market gardens for destroying pests of this kind, and although writing without personal experience, I think that it might prove useful on golf courses in cases of this sort.

Possibly there may be the luxury of water laid on to each putting green : if so, and there is sufficient pressure, the mains should be large enough to allow of two or three being watered at the same time. A night staff should be organised for this work, and the greens which are watered should receive a thorough drenching. However, if the greens are properly constructed and the grass well fed, in most localities water will not be a necessity by any means for established turf. On many links where there is no water laid on, the grass on the putting greens will be quite a different colour to the surrounding turf for a considerable time during a drought. This is the result of good feeding, and if proper attention has been paid to this, the effects of a spell of dry weather need not be much feared. It would be difficult to instance a case of properly established turf being killed in this country by drought, but, of course, this does not apply to young grass or newly laid turf.

Although it is a very simple matter to cut a golf hole, it is not always quite so easy to select the exact spot. It is advisable for medal play, or other forms of scoring competitions, to select easy places for the holes—that is to say, hollows in preference to anything in the nature of a ridge. This really affects the greenkeeper as much as the competitors. More putts are holed, and therefore, assuredly, fewer complaints made. But there is one essential to good hole-cutting—it is, that the hole-cutter be really sharp. A blunt one will never do good work, the edge of the hole will not be cut cleanly, and so will wear badly. The holes will need to be constantly moved, and if there is much play it may be necessary to do this every day. The head greenkeeper should go round his course first thing every morning to do this and to shift the tees. It is hardly necessary to say that the hole tin should be at least one inch below the surface. If tall flag-pins are needed, hollow bicycle tubes are good, provided that they have a solid spike, about eighteen inches in length, firmly fixed into the end. This spike should allow for at least nine inches purchase in the ground.

In bad weather, when the greens are likely to be damaged, the holes should be either cut on ground to the side of the regular putting greens or placed at the nearest point on the green to the tee. This will prevent a track being made across the green to the tee. If there are any subsidiary greens, it is a good plan, when frost is likely to come on, to cut holes ready for use and fill them up with a little long grass, as otherwise in the very early stages of a thaw it may be impossible to cut the holes until after the greens have been damaged. Before closing the section dealing with the maintenance of putting greens, mention should be made of the staff of men employed in this work. They should be thoroughly organised and the course divided into sections. The men should then be kept to their own particular sections. This creates a certain amount of rivalry, and a "keenness" which might otherwise be absent. On large courses where there are the necessary funds, an odd man or two is decidedly useful for work out of the ordinary routine.

The work through the green will consist of dressing any specially poor portions, rolling with horse rollers in the early spring or whenever needed, bush-harrowing and cutting the grass whenever required, either with horse mowing-machines or with hand machines with side rollers. Divot marks must be filled up with light soil with a little seed mixed with it. It may be thought advisable to graze sheep on the course—and this will undoubtedly do good if the turf is established—but, unless penned when the course is being much used, they will prove rather a nuisance, and if allowed on the putting greens their urine may scorch the grass. If there are no sheep, the expense of keeping the grass short will be heavy on most soils.

But as soon as a good covering of grass has been obtained all over the course, do not continue the use of manure and turn your golf links into suitable fattening land for bullocks. Stop using manure altogether and watch the turf carefully, and if any become poverty-stricken, then dress it. Boxes need not be used in the mowing machines unless worms begin to work freely: then probably the less humus or decayed vegetable matter that is returned to the soil so much the better.

As soon as turf is taken up from the nursery a fresh supply must be arranged for at once. But it is not a bad plan to take a crop first of early potatoes and then sow down in the following autumn. This gives an opportunity for cleaning the land, and the manure used comes in for the fresh crop of turf.

Greenkeeping is, indeed, an interesting subject for the enthusiast, and he is liable to let his opinions run away with his better judgment. Personally, I have had some twelve years' experience, and as each year goes by I see how impossible it is to make many definite or dogmatic statements as to what is right and what is wrong. There is such a vast difference in soils, temperatures, rainfalls, and many other things in different localities. Very often the soil of the same course varies largely in different parts. Each greenkeeper must, to a certain extent, work out the various little problems for himself, and he can only do this by keeping his eyes well open and trying to observe all things carefully. A considerable part of this small contribution is based upon a close study of the behaviour of the putting greens at Sunningdale in the company of my friend Hugh M'Lean, the greenkeeper there. We always have a tour of inspection at least once every week, and I think that we enjoy this work together probably more than any other during the whole of the week.

CHAPTER VI

THE CONSTRUCTION AND UPKEEP OF HEATH LAND COURSES

By W. HERBERT FOWLER

Construction.

WHEN I first saw Walton Heath there was very little to make one suppose that a first-class course could be made upon it, beyond the fact that in the few grass rides and paths was growing turf of a very fine quality. It was all covered with heather of the most robust nature, some two to three feet high, and where there was no heather there were masses of giant whins; but the drainage was good, and it is a glorious open space, with no trees or ditches, and the rolling ground is here and there broken up by chasms, which promised to make capital natural hazards. The Romans, I found, had been there some years ago, and they had designed some excellent bunkers, which I was first of all told by archæologists were used as stables for their horses, but now higher authorities say that they were camp kitchens; anyway, they come in capitally in forming the best type of hazards. You may see the same deep hollows at Huntercombe, which, no doubt, was also a Roman camp. One of the most important facts in making a golf course is to find out what the natural drainage is like, and where it is bad or indifferent it is most important to drain thoroughly before sowing the grass seed. No really good grass is grown where the drainage is bad, and it is a strange fact that the better the drainage the better the grass will stand droughts in summer, the reason, no doubt, being that in well-drained land the roots are more healthy and go deeper into the soil. At Walton we were fortunate, as the heath is situated on the chalk hills of Surrey, and though there is from six feet to twenty feet of varying soils over the chalk, still it is always perfectly dry, and even in the wettest weather never becomes really soft.

Having thoroughly examined the whole of the heath, and eventually decided to make a golf course on it, the next thing to do was to settle where to go. We had some 600 acres available, and most of the ground was very suitable, but eventually I came to the conclusion that I would go out by way of a spot which appealed to me as promising two extra good short holes, and that, in view of making the upkeep of the green easy, I would keep the outgoing and incoming courses fairly near together. I was also anxious to so arrange the holes that it should be easy to play a short round, and this

WALTON HEATH—VIEW OF BUNKERS ROUND 6th GREEN.

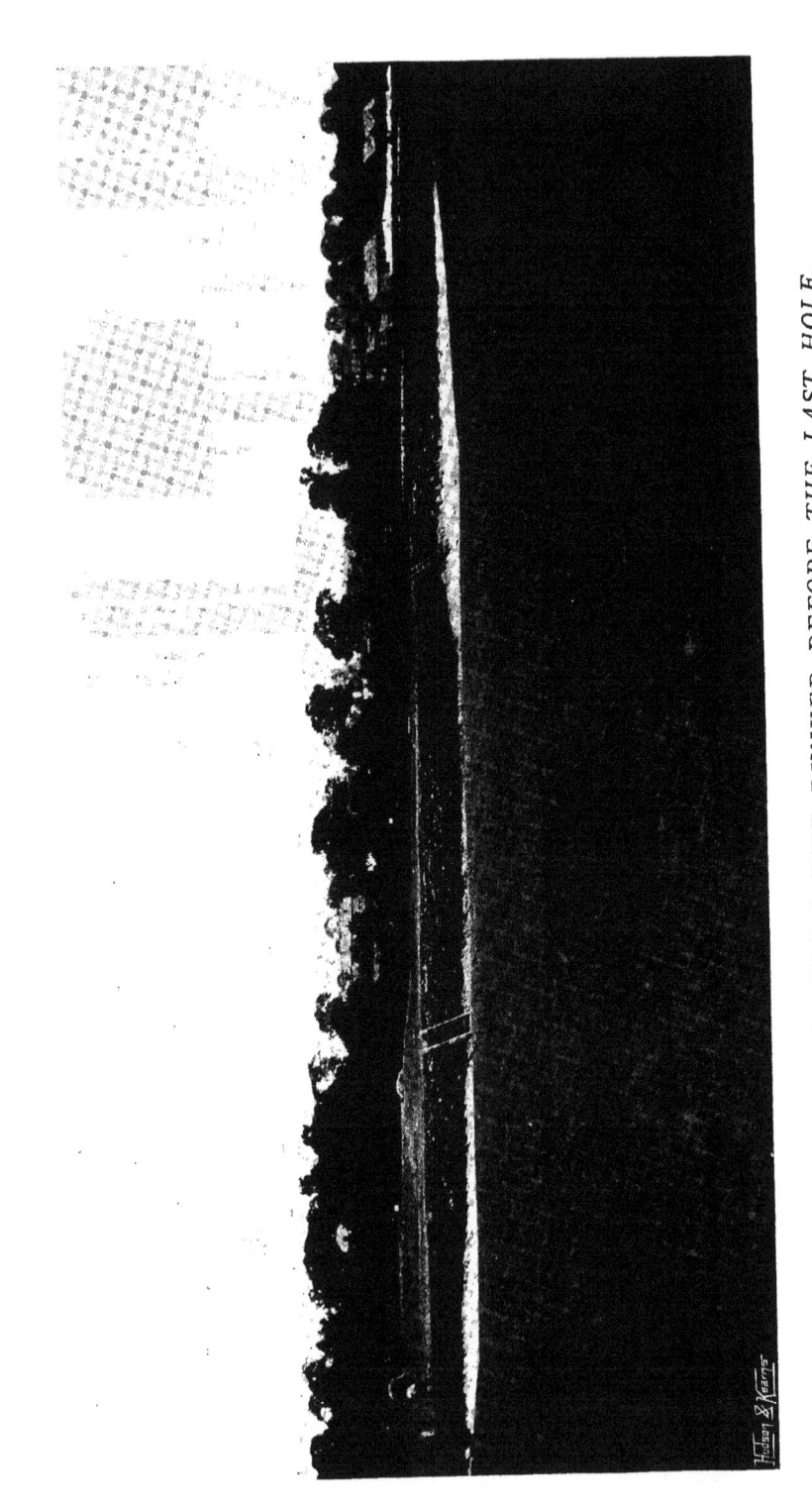

WALTON HEATH—THE LARGE BUNKER BEFORE THE LAST HOLE.

I was able to manage, and by playing the first and the last six holes a capital twelve-hole round is possible.

Having settled roughly on the spots which I thought most likely to make interesting greens, we marked out the course and set to work to cut the heather and whins. This was a big job and cost a lot of money. We could have burnt the heather, but not the whins, but I thought I should be able to sell the heather for packing pottery. But I found the demand was so limited that had I to do the work again I should burn the heather and cut the whins—that is to say, I should do so if I were going to sow seed, but I find that at Walton it is only necessary to clear the heather and keep the ground well rolled, and occasionally harrowed, for the natural grass of the country to come of itself and make a capital turf. This method would not answer everywhere, and would, of course, take somewhat longer than preparing the ground and sowing seed. Once having cleared the various growths, we employed a steam plough to thoroughly break up the ground, going to a depth of about twelve inches, and then worked it with harrows until we had got it quite clean and free from the bracken roots, which were very numerous. The top soil is a sandy loam, and in it are a number of small flints, and it took a long time to get these removed by the agency of a number of women and boys. This was a somewhat expensive process but a very necessary one, and, after all, the flints are worth something considerable for paths or roads, and it is absolutely necessary to get rid of them if one is to play golf in comfort. The next step was to work in large quantities of manure, which we got from London, as we wanted to make sure of getting a good turf in a short time, and, no doubt, all these heath lands, although they grow a fine turf, are very poor and want plenty of help. The ground was now ready for the seed, and in late August and early September we sowed twelve bushels to the acre of Dutch fescue, supplied by Messrs. James Carter & Co. This was the seed used for "through the green," but the greens were sown with fourteen bushels of a mixture of poas, fescues, and agrostis supplied by the same firm. Later on we tried an American agrostis, which has turned out extremely well, and is certainly the best winter-green seed we have had. In summer it flowers very near the ground, and as the machine does not touch the flowers it gets rather slower than the other mixture. We are fortunate at Walton in having plenty of rabbits to assist in keeping the grass short and fine, and, having got in the seed, we had to wire out the rabbits until the grass was up and the ground had become firm and solid. This took some miles of wire netting, but it was quite a necessity if the best result was to be achieved. It did not take long before the young plant began to make its appearance. By

November we had quite a nice turf, and by March we were able to start rolling it, and working daily at the greens to get them into order for playing on. We began to play in April, and in the second week of May we were able to open the course and form the Club; whilst early in June a professional tournament was largely attended, and they putted on one green which had been sown on the 1st of April previous! In addition to all the above work, we laid on water to every green and tee. This work was done by the staff on the spot, no special men being employed.

In marking out the course, I adopted the plan of clearing the course of heather to a total width of 70 yards, and of this we ploughed and sowed 50 yards, leaving the rest rough. We also left 100 yards in front of each tee just as the men left it after cutting the heather and whins, and the result is that now, in most cases, the traffic has resulted in quite a good turf coming at very little expense. Soon after play began I found that 70 yards was rather too narrow, especially in the long holes, and we have by degrees widened the course in many places, but only by cutting or burning the heather, and leaving the ground rough, so that fewer balls are lost and the time spent in looking for them is saved. I think it better in making a course in heather land to clear fairly wide and to put in bunkers to act as hazards for wide shots. Where the heather is strong it is quite likely that you may get an impossible lie, perhaps only a few feet off the line, and there is also the annoyance of losing balls, temper, and time, whilst being in a bunker is looked upon as one of the ills of golf which is to be expected.

Having arrived so far as to get the course and greens sown, we set to work to form some of the bunkers. Had I to do the job over again, I should design all the side bunkers in the greens before sowing or laying the turf, as considerable money and time is saved thereby. The bunker question is a very large one, and I propose to devote a part of this chapter to the formation and placing of hazards, but at the moment I would only say that in making a course, only side hazards should be put in during construction, any cross bunkers being left till it is seen how the ball will run when the course is finished. The advantage of making the green bunkers before sowing the seed in the greens is that very often it is necessary to form a slight bank on the green side, and if this is done before sowing it does away with lifting the turf afterwards, and altogether makes a better job. We have adopted this plan with great success in the new nine-hole course we are now making at Walton Heath.

We are fortunate at Walton in being able to go down as deep as we like in making a bunker, and in any cases where the water does not go away of itself we sink a shaft about three feet square down nearly to the chalk, and then fill it up with old pots, pans, or large flints. They are then always dry, and are much the best type of bunker.

Upkeep.

Having made a course, and play being started on it, the most important business of keeping it in good order, and from time to time making improvements on it, becomes a necessity. Greenkeeping, as at present understood, is quite a modern science, and a most interesting one too. In old days the club professional was also greenkeeper, and, of course, it often turned out that a man who was a first-class player had the most elementary ideas of different manures, grass seeds, weeds, and other matters most necessary for a competent greenkeeper to understand. But there is another and, I think, more fatal objection to a professional player being also greenkeeper, and that is that it is quite impossible for the same man to be in several places at the same time, and as it is necessary to be with the greenmen constantly to get the full value of their work, and to see that they are doing it properly, it is evident that a man who is playing with or giving lessons to members and also attending to his club-making, can only see a very little of the men employed on the green ; therefore I feel sure clubs will do well to have a man as greenkeeper who has nothing else to do.

I do not intend to discuss the whole subject of greenkeeping as a science, but only to give my experience as regards the upkeep of a course made out of heath land.

The general course requires only to be repaired from time to time by filling up holes with a little earth and sand, with some grass seed in it, and wherever any particular part looks shabby or poor by giving a dressing of earth and well-rotted manure. It is a good plan to get manure from London stables in the summer, when the ground is hard and carting does no harm, and mix it with soil of the district and leave it for some months to rot, occasionally turning it over. It can then be put on when desired, and will soon go into the grass, and be no trouble to the players. Earth and soil should never be brought from outside the district, or even from ground which, even if near by, is not of the nature of the heath, as I am sure it does more harm than good. Take the top spit from any out-of-the-way spots, and put it in heaps, and in a few months it will be ready for use.

As a rule there are rabbits on such courses, and it is well to see that their numbers are not too much reduced, as they are of immense help to the greenkeeper. They keep the grass fine, and also keep the mowing bill down. The few scrapes they make can easily be filled up, and if it is required to keep them off any particular green it is quite easy to net them out at night.

The most important part of the greenkeeper's duties is the upkeep of the greens and tees. The latter come in for the most serious wear, and, if possible, they should be made of the natural turf of the heath. This will outlast sown turf by a long time, and it also recovers much more quickly. The roughest turf of the district will make splendid tees. The upkeep of the greens is, of course, the subject which gives the greenkeeper the most trouble, and which is less understood than any other part of his duties. The pleasure of playing golf is greatly increased where the greens are so kept that putting is a true science. The turf should be not only close but fine, and the greens should be firm to the foot, and not elastic or springy, as so often is the case. To arrive at such a condition of things should be the aim of the greenkeeper. Of course, in some courses it is quite easy to get a hard, firm surface; in others much can be done by the liberal use of coarse charcoal and sea-sand. At Walton Heath our greens are naturally hard and fast, but they have shown the good effects of liberal dressings of sea-sand put on late every September. Much has been written of late about worms, and whether they should be destroyed or not, and I will not go further here than to say that I do not think a putting green should have a worm in it, but that if you destroy them you must use sea-sand liberally to do the work of aeration which they would otherwise do. Some of the fine-ground chemical manures also help in the same direction, and as I am sure that it is impossible to get heath-land greens too rich, so I believe in giving plenty of assistance to the grass. In early spring it is a good plan to give a top-dressing of well-rotted earth and manure, put on quite fine and well brushed into the grass. This will not interfere much with play, and will fill up small holes and give the grass a slight stimulant. Later on it is good to give them a mixture of chemical manures. That concocted and sold by Hamilton, the talented greenkeeper of the Royal and Ancient Club at St. Andrews, has suited our greens at Walton Heath admirably.

Mowing must be done as required, but I do not believe in setting the machines too low, and would rather mow little and often.

As to rolling, some of the old school were much against it, but personally I believe in using a light wooden roller daily. It puts a face on the greens which it is impossible to get any other way, and tends to keep the grass fine. The use of an iron roller is quite a different matter, and though there are times when its use is of the greatest advantage, yet it should be put on with great care, and when the greenkeeper is quite sure the green is just hard enough to benefit by its application.

When you have sown a green you should, if the seed is pure, start without any weeds, and the greatest care should be exercised to see that none

TH GOLF CLUB.

rt Holes (6th and 12th).

rough
ground

12th Green
+500ft

Fair Gre
+400

7th Tee

13th Tee

6th Green
+400ft

Grassy
hollows

Grassy
Hollows

⊕ Shelter

Edge of Putt'. Green

Fair Green
+300ft

Rough Ground
+200ft

Heather

+100ft

... Hollows

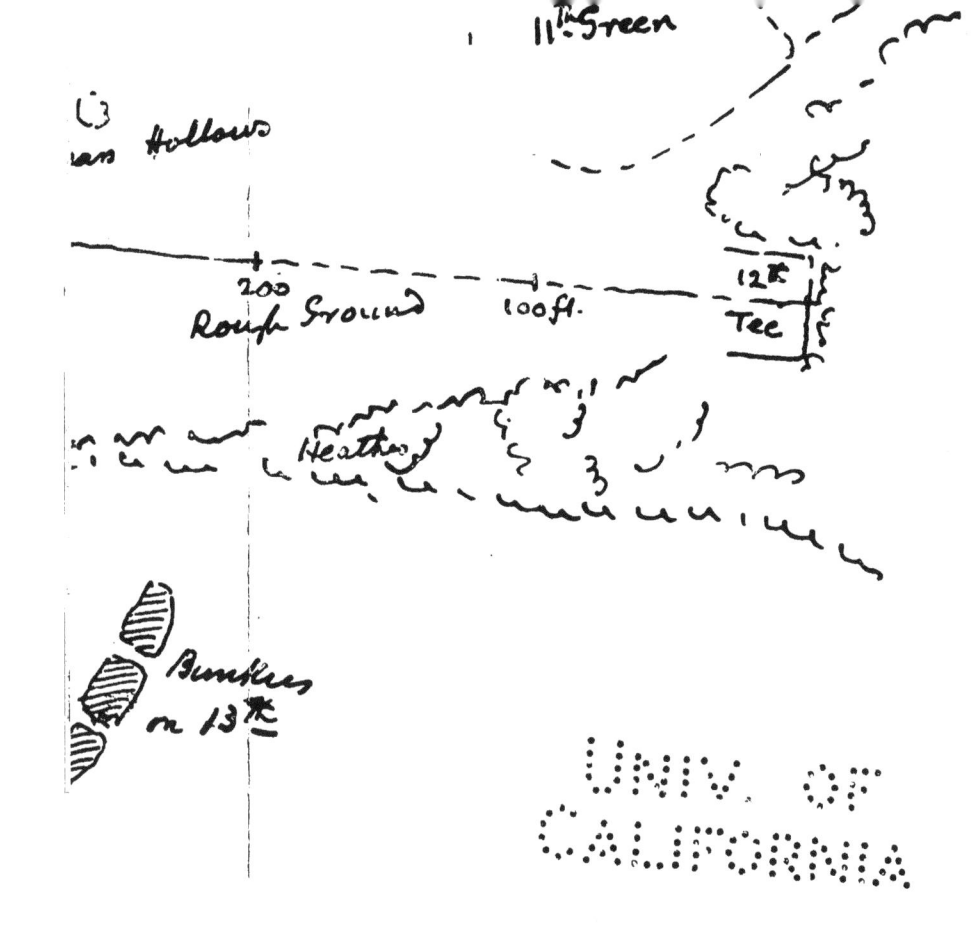

11th Green

200 Rough Ground 100 ft.

12th Tee

Heather

Bunkers on 13th

UNIV. OF CALIFORNIA

)N HEATH GOLF CLUB.

)f the two Short Holes (6th and 12th).

YING LENGTHS:
  6th Hole - 136 yards.
  12th Hole - 160 yards.

SAND BUNKERS THUS . .

are allowed to get a foothold. The difference between a green which is full of daisies or plantains and one which is all grass is enormous. Much attention has been given to this subject lately, and various compounds are sold as weed-killers, and some of them may be of use, but I believe myself that the best plan is to hand-pick the weeds, and put a pinch of seed into the hole where the weed came from.

The use of water on greens is another question which has been debated. For my part I would never pour water on a green out of a cart or by pumping from a well. If water is laid on and can be applied by pressure through a sprinkler, I am certain that its effects are wonderful in maintaining a green during a drought, but the water must be put on thoroughly, and it must be done every three or four days. At Walton Heath we have a supply to every green and tee, and when watering is necessary two of the greenmen go on to night duty, and begin watering at about six in the evening and go on all night. They generally do about four greens a night. Water should never be put on when a hot sun is shining, as this, I am sure, does more harm than good.

Bunkers should be looked after daily, and the sand kept raked well up against the face, so that impossible lies may be eliminated. On many greens the bunkers are hardly ever touched, but this is a sign of a slack or ignorant greenkeeper.

In times of snow, players often desire the greenkeeper to sweep the greens, so that play may take place. This should on no account be allowed, and I am sure that one sweeping will do more damage to a good putting green than six months' ordinary play. When snow is on the ground, golf should not be played, and the course should have a well-deserved rest; but if there is to be any play, the putting greens should be exempted. Snow does a great deal of good to grass land, as it brings down the nitrogen in the air, and acts as a fertilizer, and it also acts as a warm covering. Grass will always make growth when covered with snow, so I would say to all Green Committees, "Never mind your members, but refuse to allow a broom to be used to remove snow from a putting green." When one comes to think of what a course has to stand, it is quite wonderful how longsuffering the grass is, but I am sure that it is a good maxim to remember that if you take away you must put back. You cannot go on mowing and trampling year after year without impoverishing the grass, and if you want your course to remain good you must use plenty of dressing.

I have dealt with the subject of drainage in making the course, and will only say here that if the greenkeeper finds a green does not dry up quickly, he should put in drains at once, as it is quite impossible to grow a satisfactory turf unless the drainage is first class.

HEATH LAND COURSES

There is also the nuisance of casual water on greens, which is especially to be avoided if possible; so don't be afraid of draining. You cannot do harm by it, and most probably will do much good.

One of the important duties of the greenkeeper is the cutting of new holes as they are required. This is very often very badly done, and those in authority would do well to thoroughly explain to him that the top of a mound or a long back is not a suitable place for a hole. When important competitions are coming on, it is well to go round the day before and mark the spots with whitening so as to run no risk. After a time most men will get to know where holes should or should not be placed. It is, I think, a great mistake to keep certain spots for medal holes only. The result is that those parts of the green get less walking, and when the medal day comes round the ground all round the holes is slower and less firm than the parts of the green to which the players are accustomed.

Bunkers.

I have often thought that the importance of the hazards of a course is very much under-estimated by makers of courses, Green Committees, and players generally, and yet I think that good hazards are really almost the most important feature of a course. To my mind it is a near thing between the hazards and the greens as to which is the more vital to the making of a first-class course. There are, to be sure, all kinds of hazards, and most of them are bad : trees, hedges, ditches are all unsatisfactory, and no doubt the best are sand bunkers, so long as they are properly placed and constructed. How many courses are ruined by want of interest in the approach shot! A great deal has been written of late years about the length of the holes, and many arguments have been advanced in favour of making holes of one, two, or three full shots in length, as if this would make such holes interesting. Such theories are upset by the first strong wind that blows ; but a hole which is properly guarded can be made interesting, and as difficult as desired, by the proper placing of hazards, no matter what its length may be. In a large number of inland courses, both in the London district and elsewhere, may be found a number of greens totally unprotected on the sides : there is generally a cross hazard to be carried in a second shot, but slices and pulls are not punished. All such holes are quite wanting in interest, and I should lay it down as a maxim that the "entrance" to a green should be narrower in proportion as the length of the hole decreases: that is to say, that in short holes the entrance should be as narrow as possible, and that it should increase in width according to the average distance that the approach shot has to be played from. This practically means that unless there is some natural feature which will form the entrance, sand bunkers should be constructed, slightly in advance of the green proper, on the right and left of the entrance. Where this is done the approach shot, no matter from where played, will always be of interest, and such hazards will also govern the tee shot, and make the player endeavour so to place his tee shot that the entrance bunkers shall not be between him and the hole.

It is a curious fact that a large number of players never try to learn the proper bunker shot, and this is largely owing to the bad construction of so many inland bunkers. People who are in the habit of playing on a course where the proper bunker shot has to be played, do not find themselves so out of it when they go to the older seaside courses and find it necessary to dig the ball out of a bunker with a ten-foot face above them. Those, however, who are always playing out of shallow pans or flat bottomed bunkers get into a habit of standing too much in front of the ball, and thereby getting distance, but the ball does not rise quickly enough to enable them to get out of a deep or narrow hazard.

Formation.

All bunkers should be constructed so that the ball will roll down to the bottom, and not lie hard up against the face, and in many cases be quite impossible to get out in a line for the hole.

There should be a gradual curve from the top to the bottom of the bunker, and the deepest part should be on the side furthest from the hole. In the case of bunkers which are sunk below the level of the surrounding ground, only a few rows of turf sods are necessary, just at the top of the bunker on the side nearest the hole; but where it is necessary to construct a wall or bank, it should be built from six inches under the level of the ground up to the required height with turf sods. In places where heather grows, the best plan is to cut the heather fairly short, and then spit it out and use it as if it were turf. These heather sods make a very durable bank, and save using up turf. The bank should have a slope of about 45 degrees from the top to the lowest part of the bunker, and when filled with sand the sand should be kept raked to the slope, and if this is properly done it will prevent the impossible shots which so often occur in badly constructed bunkers. The usual bunker on inland courses has a steep bank and a flat bottom, with the result that if a ball is only just in the bunker almost any club can be used in getting it out, but if it is hard up against the face it is absolutely impossible to get it out except to one side. Most bunkers on inland greens are not deep enough. The probable reason is that on so many courses it is impossible to go any great distance below the level of the ground without getting to water, and also owing to the extra expense entailed in moving the large amount of soil necessary to excavate even a moderate-sized bunker. If the plan is adopted of making a turf wall and throwing the soil out behind it, it saves moving the excavated material and lessens the expense, but the bunker should be made on the same lines as regards the slope of the wall, etc., as if it were a deep pot sunk below the level of the ground. Of course, the wall bunker does not look so well, but it has several advantages which should not be forgotten.

In summer when the ground is hard it is wonderful how a ball will jump, and it stands to reason that a bunker made with a wall, say, four or five feet high on the side nearest the hole, will not require to be as wide as one sunk in the ground. Such bunkers are also fairer in that they are more easily seen, and, of course, they save a large sum in the original cost of making a course.

In the case of bunkers flanking a green it will be found a good plan, where it is possible to sink them below the surface of the ground, to throw out the excavated soil on the side away from the hole: this will form a bank which can be turfed, and will serve as a guide to the eye to show where the sunk bunker is situated. Such a bunker, however, to be of any real value, ought to be of considerable depth—not less than five feet, and the top should be lined with two layers of turf sods. Should bunkers be required to divide one course from another, it is a good plan to build a turf wall in the middle and excavate on both sides of it, and in such a case the wall should be five or six feet high. Unless large bunkers can be made really deep it is advisable to make a number of smaller pot bunkers, as they will cost much less to make and will be much better hazards than one large shallow bunker. Indeed, it is a waste of time and money to make a large flat bunker, like a frying-pan. I have seen many a fine brassey shot played out of such hazards, and the man who is under the face is almost unplayable.

In making bunkers it is, of course, most important to avail oneself as far as possible of any help the natural formation of the ground may give. Except in very flat ground there is generally one spot which, by reason of a natural hollow or a bank, will catch the eye as more suitable than the surrounding ground for making a bunker, and, unless such spot is obviously in the wrong place, it is well to avail oneself of its advantages, as such hazards generally look more the thing and are easier to make. For myself, I should always try and find a spot where the tendency of the run of the ball would be to lead to the bunker. This enables a smaller hazard to do the work of a much larger one, and it is only carrying out a principle which obtains on the older classic courses. It is, of course, most important to have the bunkers as dry as possible, and in many courses this is very difficult. Where a shaft can be sunk under the bunker and filled up with stone or other draining material, it will be found the most satisfactory way of dealing with the difficulty. It is almost useless to put in drain pipes, as the sand chokes them up almost immediately, and in cases where the water level in winter is near the surface, it is almost compulsory to make the bunkers by means of a turf wall above the level of the surrounding ground, but even so it should be remembered that it is not necessary to make the bottom flat. In fact, it is quite easy to make a fair hazard even if the bottom of the bunker is only a foot below the level of the ground. In such cases the turf wall must slope gradually as before, from the deepest part of the bottom, and the sand must be kept properly raked up against it. The only difference in construction will be that the turf wall will have to be higher, and as there will be less earth to dig out, the slope on the side nearest the hole will have to be much steeper than in the case of a deep bunker with a low wall. In the latter case it is best to make the slope away from the top of the wall as gentle as possible, as this gives a much better appearance than an abrupt descent.

The Placing of Hazards.

This is a subject which is constantly under discussion amongst golfers, and they are divided into two classes, viz., those who favour the cross hazards and those who consider that a side hazard to be avoided constitutes a higher test. There are certain grave disadvantages in the cross-hazard theory, and for my part I am in favour of the majority of hazards being on the sides of the course, and especially in the near neighbourhood of the green. One great difficulty in placing cross hazards is to settle how far from the tee to put them. For a tee shot one would say at once that 150 yards would be, as a rule, an easy carry for even a moderate driver, whilst for the longer player it would be very easy. But we play golf in the open, and the wind has to be reckoned with, and very often 150 yards carry will test the powers of the longest drivers when a strong wind has to be faced. As an example of this we have at the ninth hole at Walton Heath a cross bunker which is 139 yards carry, and the ground falls considerably from the tee to the hole. Very often this bunker is quite a good shot even for long drivers, and the whole of the weaker ones have to play to either side or go into it, as it is quite beyond their capacity; so that it is clear that if you put a cross hazard even 140 yards from the tee, you must, to be fair to the larger number of short drivers, give them a chance of playing a straight shot to one or other sides of it, or else you will absolutely debar them from competing at such a hole with the stronger, even if wilder, players, who are able to hit the ball further in the air. The long drivers get quite enough advantage in the course of a round by having to approach the hole from so much nearer, and I am strongly against crushing out the shorter drivers. Really, in practice it will be found that a bunker so placed as to catch the topped tee shots is all that is required, and from 100 to 120 yards is quite far enough to place a cross hazard. Where you have a long hole it is, I think, a good plan to have a cross bunker to catch a topped second shot, and these hazards also tend to make players use their heads, and decide whether they shall attempt to get over in their second shot, or play short and approach the green by a long shot from behind the bunker. On courses where the ball runs fairly well, a distance of from 300 to 340 yards will be found to be about a fair distance. With anything less than this many shots with a strong following wind will find the hazard, and the carry against the wind will not be of sufficient importance. Cross hazards guarding a green should never be put so near the hole that when the ground is hard and the wind behind, an approach shot cannot be made to stop on the green. The distance of these hazards must, of course, vary with the length of the hole and the usual distance from which the approach shot is to be played. But these hazards are only a source of trouble to the weaker players, and are really a help and a guide to the eye to the better players, and in my opinion there should only be a limited number in a round of eighteen holes. Thus I should certainly say that the best form of a cross hazard is the one to catch a bad second shot, and this only at a long hole. There are several reasons why side hazards, no matter where placed, are good, and I believe that as time goes on they will become more numerous and gain in, shall I say "popularity," with the rank and file of golfers. We all know that where one topped shot is made a very much larger number of pulls and slices are seen, and personally I think that a slice is certainly a greater fault than a top, and I would, therefore, in laying out a course, place a majority of the side hazards on the right and a lesser number on the left of the fair-way. Another point in favour of side hazards is that it is far more difficult to avoid a hazard than to carry one, and the most interesting tee shots are those where one has to make sure of passing either to one side of a hazard or between two, at such a distance from the tee that even the long drivers cannot be at all sure of carrying them. For example, the tee shots at the eighth and ninth holes at Walton Heath are fair illustrations. At the eighth there are two pot bunkers on the right and left at about 190 yards from the tee, and the ground is rising from the tee to the bunkers. How many shots find one or the other hazard! And yet there is over thirty yards between the two. At the ninth the cross hazard is 139 yards from the tee, and all the moderate drivers go at it with the greatest confidence. There is no comparison between the difficulty of the two shots. Another reason in favour of the side hazard is that it is unaffected by wind, and in case of the cross hazard a strong wind one way or the other either makes it absurdly easy or else impossible.

In placing bunkers on a course, great attention should be paid to so arranging them that they should work in with the hazards in close proximity to the green. Thus, in a hole of, say, 500 yards long, if a bunker is placed on the right of the course at, say, 380 yards from the tee, the player will have to play to pass it on the left. If a bunker is placed in the left-hand front corner of the green, it will be seen that the nearer the player can pass the right-hand bunker the less the bunker in the green will affect his approach shot. Such an arrangement will add greatly to the interest of a long hole. In fact, all bunkers should, as far as possible, be placed to govern other shots besides the actual one which is played when carrying or passing them. A good example of this is in the new bunker which has been cut in the bank guarding the fifteenth hole at St. Andrews on the old course. Formerly the line of the shot was a matter of quite secondary importance: so long as the shot was long enough to permit of getting home with the next, the line did not matter at all. Now, however, a bunker of about ten yards wide has been cut in the left-hand face of the green, and in order to be able to play the approach shot with any chance of getting near the hole it is necessary to keep the tee shot on a certain line, so that although the new bunker is some 350 yards from the tee, yet it governs the tee shot and makes the player take the greatest pains to keep his first shot on a line which will enable him to pass this small hazard and run up to the hole. The cutting of this bunker has made this one of the best two-shot holes at St. Andrews, where it was formerly one of the worst.

The placing of bunkers as guards to a green is, perhaps, the most important point to be considered in making a new course or improving an old one. So long as a green is really well guarded and the approach shot difficult, the hole will always be considered a good one, but where the main difficulties are in the tee shot and the approach is easy, the better players, at any rate, will never take the same interest in the play of it. The ideal hole, of course, should have difficulties both in the tee and approach shots, and, if possible, the hazards should be so arranged that a player having "placed" his tee shot shall play the second shot at an advantage over the player who has been wild. I have dealt with the cross hazard, and where such are employed in guarding a green, enough room must be given to stop an approach down wind. This distance must vary according to the distance from which the approach is to be played. At Walton Heath the last hole measures just 400 yards, and there is a wide bunker guarding the green about 340 to 350 yards from the tee, thus giving 60 yards from the bunker edge to the hole. This is necessary, as the approach is very often played with a full wooden-club shot, but in a hole of, say, 300 to 320 yards much less room would be required. All greens are the better for side hazards of some sort or another, and personally I am in favour of hazards behind the green too, though they are not of such importance as those on the sides. To my mind there should, if possible, be an "entrance" to all greens. By this I do not mean two bunkers, placed with mathematical accuracy exactly opposite each other on the right and left corners of the green, but that there should be a definite entrance to play for. It answers quite well and does not look so formal if one bunker is some little distance in front of the green on one side, and another start in the corner of the opposite side and takes a turn and runs some distance down the side of it. Such a bunker will have to be lofted when the approach has not been straight, and will prevent slack approaching. The width of the entrance should vary with the distance from which the approach shot has been played. When we come to the short holes I must say I think that, as a rule, they are far too easy and uninteresting. Unless there are some natural features which make them difficult, I think they should be thoroughly guarded. But, first of all, they should be really short—such a length that even against a wind the weaker players should be able to get up to the hole, say, 120 to 150 yards—but the shorter the hole is the more difficult it should be made. Such a hole should, in the first place, have a narrow green, and be guarded on both sides and behind. If there is a cross hazard, it should not be too near the green and should not be too wide. But the main point, I think, is that the green of a short hole should be absolutely defined—that is to say, that unless the tee shot comes to rest on a very moderate-sized green it is in a hazard, or a hazard has to be negotiated before the hole can be reached. How many short holes there are which have a large green and no side bunkers, and how stupid they are! Just knock the ball over the hazard and you may be thirty yards from the hole, and yet be able to play with a putter! An example of this is the fourteenth hole at Deal, where the green is large and flat, and once over the bunker a putting shot is possible from all sorts of distances. This is, to my mind, the worst hole at Deal, and Deal, I think, is the best course in England. But a very little work would make it much more interesting, and I always hope to find that the Green Committee have put in some side bunkers, and made the fourteenth worthy of its place in such a splendid course. An example of a good short hole is the eleventh at St. Andrews. It is quite possible to put the ball all the way and run no risk, but what a terrifying shot it is, especially when a strong cross wind is blowing! The deep bunker to the left and that horrid pot called " Strath " on the right, and such a narrow space between the two; but what a satisfaction to see the well-played shot, and the ball lying on the green near the hole! Why not dead? How many good medal scores has this short hole ruined, just because one thinks one must play for a three! It can be made a certain four, but it is there, looking at one so invitingly. Woe betide the ball which is pulled into the deep left-hand bunker, or that is too strong and in the Eden! Of course, in inland greens it is very difficult to get such holes, as it is rare to find the ground which would lend itself to such a scheme; but much can be done, and the sixth, or " Port Arthur," at Walton Heath is an example of a good inland short hole. In fact, it would be considered a good hole anywhere. It is narrow and well guarded, and quite open. I hold that wherever possible no *approach* shot or short hole should be *blind*. A blind tee shot may pass muster, but when approaching, the hole should, if possible, be visible; and this is specially the case in a short hole. Half the pleasure in playing a shot at short range is to watch the course the ball takes after it has touched the ground, and to note the good or bad treatment it receives. Another point in favour of the visible hole is that it gives strangers on a course a much better chance of competing against a player with "local knowledge."

Only general advice can be given as to the placing of bunkers on a course, and certain leading principles which should be observed. Much must always depend upon the formation of the ground and natural features, and the arrangement of the bunkers should vary slightly at the different holes so as to avoid monotony; but the main point to aim at should be fairness to all classes of players, and putting a premium on straightness and accuracy as against length.

CHAPTER VII

FORMATION AND UPKEEP OF COURSES MADE OUT OF PINE FORESTS

By Mr. S. Mure Fergusson

To anyone who has been accustomed to play golf on a seaside course the idea of making a links in a pine forest seems, to say the least of it, a curious one. But when one thinks the matter out it is not so peculiar, for most pine forests grow on sand, and for a golf links sand is a *sine qua non*, at least from my point of view. There are many inland courses where golf is played and enjoyed on which sand is unknown, but to the golfer who has played chiefly on sea courses the want of sand entirely changes the game. During some parts of the year these sandless courses are a fair imitation of the real thing, but directly hot or wet weather arrives the course is either dried up or so muddy that play is no longer a thing to be desired, and I doubt very much if the true golfer would take the trouble to play were it not for the exercise the game gives. To return to the subject of this article, viz., how to make a golf course out of a pine forest, I fancy the few following remarks may assist anyone desiring to achieve this end:—

The forest must not be too thick or too flat, as the undulations of the ground are necessary to make it interesting. Also, it is important to examine the ground closely for any sign of turf, and I need hardly say that this turf will not be discovered unless there may happen to be a few rides running through the pines. As a rule, one will find the turf on these rides the right sort for a golf course, viz., short and crisp, owing to the pedestrian traffic and the nibbling of that useful little animal, the rabbit, which loves to feed on this sort of pasture. Given the existence of this turf and a certain amount of undulation in the ground, the formation of the course is merely a matter of engineering and money.

The first thing to be done is to have a plan made of the area over which the course is to extend, and, having settled this, the next thing is to arrange the holes according to the orthodox lengths of an ordinary golf course, keeping in view any natural hazards there may be. The intitial work to be put in hand, after choosing the sites for the proposed putting greens, is to prepare the ground by clearing away the trees, etc., and then the ground should be got into order by putting about eighteen inches of good soil over the space cleared. In the meantime, turf taken from the rides or obtained somewhere in the district should be cut and stacked ready for

COURSES MADE OUT OF PINE FORESTS 121

laying down directly the ground has been prepared. As soon as the turf has been laid (and this should be done in the early autumn before the frost arrives), it should be rolled, first of all, with a heavy roller, and as soon as it is set should be rolled constantly with a light roller until the surface becomes fairly level. If this has been done in the early autumn, I should then cover the whole of the green with ordinary London manure, which will keep the frost out during the winter, and will also stimulate the growth directly the spring arrives. The grass should be allowed to grow until it becomes fairly firm, and then should be constantly cut and rolled till it assumes the guise of a natural putting green. If any part of the green so made should look poor, I should encourage it with a little bone dust manure, taking care that it is not put on too thickly, as this is apt to produce too thick a grass. The great aim, in my opinion, is gradually to get the made greens to assume the same appearance as the turf on the rides aforementioned. If there are not too many rabbits they will do no harm; on the contrary, they will feed down the greens, and very little cutting will be necessary.

Having finished the greens, they should be watered through the summer, if a dry one, by placing American sprinklers on the ground, and letting them throw the water throughout the night.

The next thing to do is to clear off the trees

from the proposed ground between the holes, and this should be done by tearing the trees out of the ground by means of a steam engine, so that the roots of the trees are not left. When a clearance has been made, say about 80 yards in breadth, the ground should then be prepared for sowing grass seed, which can be obtained from Messrs. Carters or any seed merchant, who would send down a man to examine the existing grasses, and provide the proper sort of seed. Probably a considerable portion of the ground so sown may not show good results, and if so, far the best plan, in my opinion, is to turf with the turf of the district from a nursery, which should always be kept well provided with lots of stacked turf. This will soon set, and by judicious rolling and watering the result will be much more satisfactory than on the part which has been sown. Of course, to turf the whole course would be out of the question, but turfing should be done wherever the grass does not come up well the spring after it has been sown. Probably during the first year or so a lot of moss will appear, but this will soon be stamped out by the constant walking over the course, and if it should appear in quantities, as it often does in the winter, a dose of soot should be given, and by the spring it will be gone. I am not in favour of having trees as hazards to drive over as a rule, and they should be avoided, as they make a bad hazard and are foreign to the game. Also, the course should not be made

COURSES MADE OUT OF PINE FORESTS 123

too easy by taking out too many trees and making the fair-way between the holes too broad. Straight driving is very important, and from 60 to 80 yards broad is quite enough. If the course lends itself to heather, so much the better, as I should leave 70 or 80 yards of the ground in front of the teeing greens rough, and simply top the heather when it gets too high.

Having so cleared and sown the seed and turfed the bad bits, the ground should be constantly rolled by not too heavy a roller, and after a year or eighteen months the course should be good enough to allow of a little play. No bunkers should be cut until the ground has become more or less firm, as only then can the distances of the drives be reckoned and the knowledge of where to place the bunkers be gained. If the bunkers are made before the ground has become firm, they are sure to be put in the wrong places, and the work of making them will have to be all done over again. As most pine forests grow on sand, the making of the bunkers is very easy work, and should be done by digging the ground out below the surface, and making a bank at the back of the bunker about two to three feet high according to the position of the hazard. The bank should be made by sods of turf being laid on top of each other at the back of the bunker, and in time, after people have walked over them and played out of the bunkers, they will assume a natural aspect and lose the artificial appearance they may have at first. Nothing, to my mind, is more abominable on a golf course than the awful zarebas that used to be erected by poor Tom Dun and others who first laid out inland greens. The bunkers should not be too deep, and should always have a sloping bank towards the hole, so that if one gets in and can play the shot as it ought to be played, one can play towards the hole and not sideways or back as is often the case in artificial bunkers. One of the most skilful shots at golf is the shot out of a bunker, but if the face is perpendicular and seven or eight feet high, as is the case on some links—take Walton Heath for example—it becomes a farce, for one cannot play towards the hole, and any fool can play out sideways. The bunkers should also not be made too narrow, and should take the form of pots if placed near the hole. A long, straggling bunker across the course is not a good thing, for in a gale of wind the sand is apt to be blown out, and necessitates constant refilling. A sand pit should be dug in some part of the course where sand would be always available.

To return to the putting green for a moment, sand should be freely spread over the young grass, as nothing tends to produce fine grass more than the constant use of sand.

In my opinion a golf course made out of a pine forest is more quickly got into playing order than almost anywhere else, as, the soil being light and free from clay, one is not bothered by wet weather. Speaking of the New Zealand course near Byfleet as an example, I have seen the whole surrounding country under water, but when one got on the course it was as dry as bone. Of course, ditches and drains must be cut where necessary. Another advantage of such a course is that gorse, broom, heather, and all sorts of small flowers grow all over the course, and are a source of great pleasure to the eye in spring and summer, whilst the scent from the pines is delicious. In bad weather, too, the presence of trees is very welcome, as they afford shelter from the wind and rain. I do not say for a moment that a course so laid out is the pleasantest for an erratic player, but it is an excellent school, and teaches one to keep straight, though it sometimes hampers the player who delights in long driving.

After the course has been laid out, the most important facts to remember are the constant rolling throughout the year with a fairly heavy horse roller until play becomes general, when the mere tramping of the feet will be almost enough; the constant rolling and sanding of the putting greens; and the filling up with sand of the divots taken out by the iron play. The brooms used for sweeping the greens should be quite light, and should be in the shape of a fan made of twigs. If the greens should become bad owing to worm casts, there is a preparation which, if put on diluted with water in proper quantities, will soon get rid of them. The effect of it is that the worms come up in thousands, and they are then swept away by the light brooms.

I am afraid the information I have given may not be very complete, but it may help anyone who contemplates the really not very formidable task of laying out a golf course in a pine forest.

CHAPTER VIII

TREATMENT OF AN INLAND GREEN
ON MEDIUM SOIL

By PETER LEES

MY experience as a greenkeeper extends over a period of about twenty years, both on seaside and inland courses, and I think I can safely claim to have served a pretty fair apprenticeship, and in the following short article I will try to explain some of the methods I employ in keeping my course and putting greens in good playing condition all the year round; but it must be understood that I do not intend my remarks to be taken as hard-and-fast rules to be followed by other greenkeepers, but simply as what I have myself found out from my own personal experience gained by actual work in the keeping of the courses I have had charge of during that time.

There can be no doubt that within the last twenty years the game of golf has made rapid strides. Golf courses have sprung up everywhere, and the art of greenkeeping has attained a very high standard of excellence, as, for a club with a course of its own nowadays to hold its own in the golfing world, everything must be kept in the very best possible condition, so that the greenkeeper now is a much more important individual than he used to be in the old days, when anybody was considered good enough to cut a fresh hole on the morning of a competition, or fill in a hole with a handful of sand. The greenkeeper now must be a man who thoroughly understands his work; and to be a successful greenkeeper he must study the nature of the soil under his charge, and find out what is best suited to keep the turf in good playing condition; and I am of opinion that he requires to be himself a player, as he can better understand what is required by golfers in general.

Well, to begin at the beginning, I will give a few of my own experiences in the upkeep of "through the green," that is, between the holes. On most inland greens the idea seems to be to get it rolled as firm and flat as possible, so that good lies may be had. But this is a fatal mistake, as I have found courses where the surface was once fine and dry turned into one of nothing but mud, and simply because the ground had been rolled with far too heavy a roller, and rolled when it was too wet on the surface. I never use a horse roller unless the surface of the ground is in condition, and never when it is raining. A good time to use the iron roller is after frost, when the ground is nice and open. In wet weather I use a horse roller made entirely of wood, and weighing about 7 cwts., as I find this

GOOD BUNKERS.

TYPICAL INLAND COURSE—CASSIOBURY.

is quite sufficient to smooth down the surface, and at the same time gathers up all worm casts, etc., and keeps the ground nice and clean. Never roll with a heavy roller unless the surface is dry, as, no matter how nice and free the ground may be at the beginning, in course of time it will entirely change, and a muddy, dirty, sticky surface will most assuredly take its place, will not be worth playing upon in winter, and in summer will be as hard as cement.

Now comes the most important part of the greenkeeper's work—the care of the putting greens. The same things apply to them as regards rolling, but only to a greater extent, as, on inland greens especially, the trouble is to keep them in good playing condition during the winter months, and too much rolling I consider the worst thing possible for them. The way I treat my greens is—I give them first a good dressing of charcoal well rubbed in with the back of an iron rake, and when I have it all out of sight, I give it another top-dressing of good sharp sea-sand, and rub that in in the same way. This dressing is the best, I think, for toning down the quality of the grass to what is required for a first-class putting green, and it at the same time creates a new surface entirely of a fine light nature, and allows the grasses to thicken up from the root, so that, in a very short time, instead of a rough, uneven green, full of holes, over which the ball jumps about when played, there is formed a splendid close carpet of excellent turf, a pleasure to play on, and the player has only himself to blame if he fails to get his ball to the bottom every time.

It is absolutely necessary, if the greens are to stand the wear and tear of play all the year round, that they should be of considerable size, so that the hole can be shifted well about and not kept always near the same place, and so that the different parts get a rest, and do not get worn out. I roll them with a light wooden hand roller, but before doing so I see that they are lightly brushed all over, so that all loose obstacles are removed. If I think they require it, I give them a roll, perhaps once a fortnight, with a light iron roller, but never unless the ground is dry on the top. I never use artificial manure on my greens, as I have learned from experience that the best top-dressing for them is a mixture of good rolled manure, rich mould, and a quantity of lime. If this is well turned over in a heap several times, and applied to any poor and sickly part, it puts some lasting good into the ground, and does not rush the grass away soft and unable to stand any wear. For seaside greens I consider that this is the best top-dressing possible, and it ought to be more used than it is, as the soil is mostly of a poor quality, and requires feeding with something substantial and lasting. There is another top-dressing I use if I want a quick result, and that is malt culms, but I always try if possible to do with the other top-dressing. But if grass is wanted quickly this malt dressing is the best I have ever tried. It is simply wonderful how it rushes on the grass. I top-dress at any time of the year, but if the weather is dry I water it in. The sea-sand and charcoal I put on from the middle of September to the end of October, as I find this the best time for this work. I mow my greens in summer as close as I can set the machine, and never let the grass get the least long. I consider the cut grass, if left on, a good manure, so I never have a box on, but always let the cut grass remain. My reasons for mowing the grass short are, first, that I find the closer and oftener it is done the thicker a carpet of turf is obtained, as the roots send up more young shoots; and, secondly, I have learned from experience that the firmer and closer your turf is the less chance the sun has to get at the roots and burn it up. I do not believe in letting it get longer in dry weather, as it does more harm than good, for the reasons I have given.

I now come to another matter which affects the inland greenkeeper more than the seaside one, that is the question of worms, and I will be as brief and to the point with this subject as possible. On inland greens after they have been in play a few years the greenkeeper will find that where at first he had only a few worms, they have multiplied to such an extent that they have become an absolute nuisance, and he must now think of some means of getting rid of the pests. Opinions differ as to the advisability of killing the worms out, but my honest opinion is that it is impossible to have a good, firm, healthy turf, such as is desired on a putting green, if the worms are allowed to throw up their casts all over the surface, as no matter how carefully they are brushed off there are a certain number left, and these in course of time, with the continued rolling that is required to make the green at all playable, form themselves into a muddy paste, with the result that the finer grasses in time get killed out, and bare patches appear. So I say (and I am speaking from experience), kill them out.

If any proof of my argument is required, my greens here are testimony of the necessity of removing the worms, as I have as fine, clean greens in winter as in summer, and they are played on seven days a week all the year round, and never get a rest, nor do they require it, because my turf is in a healthy condition. There are a number of worm killers on the market, but the most effective, and at the same time simple and absolutely harmless to the grass, is the one supplied by Messrs. Carter & Co., High Holborn, London. Some of the greens I cleared in October, 1904, and at present, in the summer of 1906, there is no sign of the worms coming back, and the grass is of a beautiful, healthy, close, firm texture.

I could go on further on the subject, but I think these few remarks will give some idea of my mode of working; but before closing, there is just one other thing I would mention, and it is the appearance of weeds in a green, and my experience of this is that when weeds appear the greenkeeper must know that something is wrong, and must set about rectifying it. From what I have learned from observation the two causes of weedy greens are too much rolling and the want of nourishment. Keep your turf healthy, feed it, and do not on any account use the roller when the surface is wet, for the finer grasses are sure to get killed out by rolling, and these are the ones that are required to make a good, true, playing green, such as will please the most fastidious golfer.

CHAPTER IX

THE UPKEEP OF A GOLF COURSE ON CHALK DOWNS

By Mr. LEONARD KEYSER

AFTER a golf club has been started, and the rules of the club drawn up, a common omission from the rules is the definition of the powers that the Green Committee should possess, and the body to which they should be responsible. At first, all may go well and smoothly, and the moving spirits who called the club into being may be the members who can best serve the interests of the club; but it must be remembered that a club grows, and often grows fast, and that members like to have matters conducted in a business-like way, and prefer that the powers of the executive should be clearly defined. If the Green Committee are appointed by the General Committee to look after the course, it stands to reason that they become a sub-committee of the General Committee, and the General Committee can call upon them never to incur any expense or undertake any work without their consent, and cases have occurred where the General Committee have so acted that a Green Committee have lost all power, and could only act as the mouthpiece of the General Committee. It is as well, then, in drawing up rules, that the duties and responsibilities of the Green Committee should be laid down. The plan which appears to work best is that at the annual general meeting of the club three members be chosen to act as the Green Committee for the year, that they should be given the entire control of the course, and should be responsible to the club for their actions, while a limit should be put upon the amount they have the power to spend. At the end of their year of office they should draw up a report of the work done, expressly stating how the several greens have been treated and dressed, and suggesting from their experience the work necessary for the ensuing year. If these reports are filed year by year they will be a guide and a help to those who follow in the office. A Green Committee being formed, it is next essential that one of their members be chosen to represent them to give the orders to the men working on the green. Men work better when they have a recognised master, and nothing is more calculated to upset good men than having to take orders from many masters.

In many clubs at the present time the club-maker and professional no longer has the charge of the green, and this practice seems to work better than the old one. If the club is prosperous the professional's whole time is taken up in clubmaking, giving lessons, or playing with members. It stands, then, to reason that he has not the time to superintend the labour on the green. Again, a clubmaker may be a past-master of his craft and also an expert golfer without any knowledge of turf and the making and preserving of greens. It seems, then, to be the better plan for the Green Committee to engage the services of a reliable greenkeeper, who has a good knowledge of turf, grass seeds, manure, etc., who is a good worker himself, and accustomed to have men working under him. It is preferable that he should have some knowledge of the game, but it is astonishing how soon an intelligent man picks up the requirements of a golf course. Such persons are to be found, and an advertisement will always be answered by men competent to take charge of a green.

The present writer has been asked particularly to give the result of his experience in the upkeep of a golf course on a chalk down. The first noticeable thing, in his opinion, is that the greens laid right down on the chalk do better than raised ones. Where much soil has been placed, and the turf laid on, the greens become spongy in wet weather, the grass grows coarsely, and as good a surface is not obtained as when the turfs are laid close down on the chalk with no artificial soil in between. Such greens are faster and truer, there is no chance of sinking, and they are altogether more satisfactory. The dressing of the greens must naturally be the result of experiments, but where the worms are too active the grass grows too coarsely, and it is difficult to get a true, hard surface. Excellent results have been obtained from the use of the SP. charcoal. This should be applied two, three, or even four times a year during wet weather. The finer powdered charcoal is not so efficacious. As the SP. charcoal is coarse, it interferes with the putting; it is therefore advisable to dress half of a green at a time, and after the charcoal has worked in, to dress the other half. Sea-sand is always good as a dressing, but building-sand does no good whatever. Where the grass becomes at all poor, or weeds prevail, any of the artificial manures as sold by the leading seed merchants are as a rule beneficial, but an overdose of artificial manure is not to be risked. Perhaps the best dressing of all is the ashes obtained from burning dead leaves. Plantains must be attacked unceasingly —they must be given no quarter and no rest; spasmodic efforts are useless: the war against them must be waged ruthlessly and continuously. The plan which seems to answer best is to dig the plantain out with a fork, with as much of its roots as possible, and to fill in the hole thus made with a mixture of fine soil, good grass seed, and artificial manure. The skill of the greenkeeper is shown in his knowledge of how much or how little rolling a green requires. Too much rolling is as great an error as too little. In winter, only the very lightest roller should be used, and not even that if frost is coming out of the ground. The long bamboo rod, if well applied, will be found very serviceable in removing worm casts and dead leaves. The hard-and-fast rule may be laid down not on any account to roll greens on chalk downs in winter with a heavy roller. Let the new tees be made in October, and do not let them be played upon before the following spring, by which time the turfs should be well knit together. Through the course worm casts should always be scattered, winter or summer. Here again the bamboo rod is excellent, even better than the bush harrow. Tees should be rested if possible after hard frost. When the frost is coming out of the ground, tees and greens are in their most delicate state, and during such time temporary tees should be used and the holes made on the near edge of the green. Caddies should not be allowed to stand all round the hole with their heavy boots; and, finally, it should be suggested to the hon. secretary of the ladies' golf club that high heels do really make bad holes on soft putting greens!

March should be devoted entirely to rolling the course. All March and April the course should be rolled again, again, and yet again. The best roller is, of course, a water ballast roller, so that the weight can be adjusted to suit the conditions of the ground. The very best weather for rolling is after and during a good drying wind, when the soil does not adhere to the roller. The present writer was once very daring. He induced the committee of the club he served to allow him to have the whole course rolled with a steam roller. The experiment was an unqualified success, and the course was improved thereby in an extraordinary way. It was delightful to watch the hummocks and inequalities being flattened out by the great weight of the roller. It need hardly be added that this rolling was done in dry weather towards the end of March.

Artificial hazards are always unsatisfactory, and it is difficult to devise anything of the nature of a hazard except the ordinary pot-bunker. Anything which grows is always destroyed by play, and such hazards as whins do not last. Mounds answer in a way. They attract the eye, and give the stroke to be played the appearance of being more difficult than it really is. To place sand in bunkers is very expensive, and on chalk downs it soon disappears into the chalk, so that such a proceeding may be dismissed as impracticable. The better plan is to rake over the bunkers continually, remove the stones, and fill the bottom with a few inches of sifted soil. Other things have been tried, but no success as yet has attended the efforts at improvement. The present writer could describe very much to his own satisfaction how numerous the bunkers on a course should be, and the position they should be placed in, but he fears the Editor's power of sarcasm, and will refrain.

The successful upkeep of golf links depends upon the labour employed upon them and the constant and daily attention which they receive. Months of neglect cannot be made up for by a great effort to recover lost ground. The work should be laid out in advance, and carried out in a systematic way. One very important piece of work is to keep cut and rolled the approaches to the greens. The greens should not be—as they are in some courses—oases in the middle of rough ground; but there should always be a fair-way to the hole, which should be kept cut and rolled as carefully as the green itself. It is a common error to think that all the labour on a course must be expended on the greens and the tees. The course itself requires just as much attention. Unless the lies through the green are good, golf is a toil and not a pleasure. It need hardly be pointed out that good lies do not come of their own accord on an inland course, but must be the result of care and attention. During the summer months the whole of the labour should be directed to keeping down the grass through the green, and for this a good horse mower is indispensable. It is better that the mower should move on wheels, as then the inequalities in the ground are better overcome. Where it is not possible to employ a horse mower, the "Pennsylvania" hand mower should take its place. It is quite surprising how much ground a good workman can cover in a day with one of these. They are very handy, too, where much turning has to be done round the bunkers and the approaches to the green. All pleasure in the game during the summer months depends upon a good fair-way being kept, and money is well spent in procuring this result. If the grass be constantly cut, it is unnecessary to remove the cut grass. When the tees became very greasy, it is a good plan to have some good stout cocoanut matting laid down, but this mat should be movable, and not fixed. If well weighted with lead at two edges it will be flat enough. The mistake often made is to have these mats too small.

To sum up, success in the upkeep of any golf links requires care, attention, and keenness on the part of the greenkeeper and the member or members deputed by the committee of the golf club to supervise and direct his work. With these three qualities, and a committee and members who will always assist and encourage all efforts which are being made, the result will be a well-cared-for course, which is really the goal to aim at where natural advantages are relatively wanting.

CHAPTER X

THE GOLF COURSE ON HEAVY SOIL

By JAMES BRAID

HAVING laid out the course to the best advantage with the ground at your disposal, the first item in the making is to see to the draining. This is such an important point that it must be done thoroughly. The best method is to cut open ditches where they do not interfere with the play. Through the lines of play and on the putting greens drains must be put in about 15ft. apart, and from 18in. to 24in. deep. Provided this has been carried out thoroughly, the drains will act for a number of years, and the course should be fairly dry and playable even during a wet season.

The next part to be attended to is the putting greens. Provided the soil is fairly good, this may not prove a very expensive item, as it is wonderful how soon rough grass will become good with judicious cutting and rolling and dressing.

It is essential that weeds should be eradicated as much as possible. This is best done by taking them out altogether, which, although a very tedious job, is the most effective. Then fill up the holes that are left with seed and soil.

The grass through the course on this kind of soil is generally strong enough to do without stimulant of any kind, the difficulty, as a rule, being to keep it short enough.

We will now proceed with the placing of the bunkers. This requires a great deal of careful thought, and all conditions of weather must be taken into consideration before coming to any conclusion. Personally, I believe in the side hazard as being the fairest, and also calling for the most accurate play, especially near the putting greens, which, as a rule, are not made difficult enough, and require drawing in a lot. Bunkers placed on the right and left of the course, 150 yards to 180 yards from the tee, are much more likely to catch a ball not hit quite fair than a cross hazard at about 120 to 130 yards off. Of course, the chief point in making these bunkers is to get as great a variety as possible. Of course, too, it is necessary to have the ground fairly rough for about 100 yards in front of the tee, so that a topped stroke will meet with due punishment. An argument very often advanced is that a very bad shot is not always punished; but this is not the case if the hazards have been properly placed, as the very bad shot will have made the next one much more difficult to negotiate, and, after all, it is much better to place hazards so as to catch the many shots which are not quite good rather than the few very bad ones.

It is always necessary to raise the banks of the bunkers, and this should be done so as to make them look as natural as possible. The reason for this is that if you dig the bunkers any depth they are sure to be always full of water in the winter.

I think a water hazard is a good hazard, as it always tests the abilities of the players, especially if the hole is immediately beyond it.

Trees, I consider, make a bad hazard, and they should he done away with where possible. Besides, they are always a nuisance when the leaves are falling.

If play is to be a pleasure, it is necessary to get rid of the worms on the putting greens. What I have found answer this purpose best is Walker's SP. charcoal, which can be applied any time between September and April, but the earlier in the autumn the better. This preparation, being of a gritty nature, does not in any way interfere with the drainage, but rather improves it than otherwise. Another very good preparation is Carter's "Worm Destroyer," which must be applied in wet weather, when the worms are near the surface, to get the best results. This preparation may have a slight pull over the former, as it does not make it necessary to stop play on the greens, while with the first named you cannot play on the greens for at least two months.

An occasional dressing of sea-sand helps very

much to improve the surface of the green and to fine down the grass, thus making the greens run much quicker.

When a green requires renovating, provided it can be shut off for some time, I would prefer to dress it with well-rotted stable manure mixed with the very best soil procurable. This should be got locally if possible, but it is essential to see that it is clear of weeds. If it is possible to close the green, Hamilton's or Carter's chemical manures are both very good and very reliable preparations. These are best applied in the spring, in the month of April.

During the winter months a great deal of damage is done by rolling with heavy rollers, which is a great mistake, the best results being obtained by running over the greens in the morning with a light wooden roller, which picks up any worm casts lying about, and does not flatten them down like a heavy one—giving the golfer the impression of playing on some flattened-out mud.

I am not in favour of sheep on a course of this kind, as they usually knock all the bunkers to pieces, and, as a rule, eat all the grass on the putting greens instead of anywhere else. During the wet weather they make so many marks that more often than not the player has quite an unplayable ball.

Rabbits, as long as they do not become too numerous and scrape too much on the greens, are rather an advantage than otherwise, as they nibble the grass nice and short, without tearing it out by the roots.

Through the course, from the month of April until October, not much else is required but the constant use of the mower. The difficulty always is to keep the grass short enough. During the winter months the occasional use of a bush harrow, when the ground is dry enough, will improve the lies. Rolling must be abstained from, as it prevents the water from getting away.

CHAPTER XI

MAKING A PARK COURSE

By E. Mepham

THE best time for making a course in a park is between October and March. The rough grass should be mown with a scythe as soon as the rainy season sets in, as it cuts much easier than when it gets older. Then the small hollows should be heaved up with a digging fork instead of taking off the turf, the edges eased into the centre with same, and then rammed down firm with a wooden rammer. The mounds, such as ant heaps, if any, should be levelled by taking off the turf first and then the soil above the level. Replace turf and ram down firm and then roll. I have found a pony roller $2\frac{1}{2}$ feet wide and 7 cwt. 3 qrs. in weight very useful for this work, but the pony must have boots on, or the ordinary rubber pads, which answer the purpose of boots and are better for the pony. I have used them winter and summer instead of the hot, leather boots. For making nine approaches this way the cost would be about £15 15s.

Greens.

Where greens have to be levelled the turf should be taken off in squares of 12 to 15 inches, not rolled as lawn turf, and $1\frac{1}{2}$ inches thick. The mould should be taken up and wheeled on one side, the under soil levelled as desired, and then well rammed to prevent its sinking uneven. Drain with pipes 12 to 18 inches deep. The drains could be half filled with stones next to the pipes, and finished with light mould, as this drains much quicker than close soil. Then spread the mould that has been wheeled aside over the green about four inches deep, replace turf, ram, and roll even. Then a good top-dressing of light mould mixed with a little grass manure should be worked in with a broom when dry enough. This dressing fills all the little crevices and gives the grass a good start. For making a green in this way, 16 yards square, the cost would be about £10.

When a green lies very wet, a good plan is to loosen the soil about nine inches deep, and mix light sandy mould by spreading mould first and then breaking the soil up with a pick so as to mix it thoroughly together. Then ram down firm to keep it from sinking. This process helps to drain a green, but it must be drained with pipes as well.

Natural Greens.

Natural greens should be mown close, the small mounds taken away, and the hollows filled up by taking off turf and filling up with mould. After this, replace turf, and ram and roll down firm. Bare places should be turfed, not seeded. Top dress as above described. The cost of making a green in this way would be about £4.

Keeping of Greens.

I think the most important part of green keeping is the feeding of greens. I have always used mould of different kinds, as it is best suited to make up for what is worn and swept off. It forms a covering for the roots of the grass and encourages a new growth both of root and grass, sustains the greens through winter, and saves a deal of watering in summer. The moulds that I have used are composed of turf mould, leaf mould, and sand, and a little grass manure mixed is very good for a change. Turf mould and stable or farmyard manure make a good mixture, and sometimes mould and wood ashes. The dressings should be different, not the same, season after season, as a change improves grass and brings a better growth. The best time to apply is in early spring. If the greens are dry, a good brushing with a stable broom prevents moss and freshens the surface of the green, but where greens are mossy, dressing with these moulds and working on them is the best remedy that I have found. The dressing should be screened through a fine sieve and worked in with a broom and rolled when dry. If applied as the grass begins to grow, it prevents the green drying so hard after the winter's rolling.

Rolling.

There is a great difference in greens as to rolling—a damp one wants much more than a dry one, but where there is a lot of play they need less. Of course, rolling does a lot of good, as well as treading, in the way of bringing fine grass and keeping the greens even. For an instance of this, look at grass paths and sheep tracks: the grass is always short and green and free from moss. But too much rolling does harm as well as good. A park course, however, wants a fair amount. Care should be taken to remove all worm casts before rolling greens, especially with an iron roller, or it flattens them down and causes bare places. Old farmers would tell one that rolling grass when the ground is sodden does as much good as a coat of manure. The same remark may be applied to greens, but the rolling must not be done too often.

Sweeping.

Sweeping of greens is necessary every morning where sheep and rabbits feed on them, but they should be swept as lightly as possible so as not to injure the grass. The harder the green is swept in winter the poorer and more bare it gets, and, again, it should always be swept one way, for if sometimes swept one way and then another it roughens the grass and makes the greens much slower. They should not be swept down hill if slanting, but crossways, as sweeping downhill causes the grass to lie that way, and makes the greens very fast down and slow up.

Mowing.

Some greens want much more mowing than others, but if there should be sheep, or deer, or rabbits feeding on them, it is better for the grass and requires less mowing. Again, feeding is better than mowing: the grass is fed shorter, and has to break direct from the roots, and so comes closer and finer, and is even all over. Where it is only mown the mounds are cut much shorter than the hollows, so that one place is fast and another is slow. Where greens are heavy with too much grass, it should be taken off when mown, but where they are dry and fast it should be left on, as it protects the green in hot weather and saves watering.

Destroying Worms.

Destroying the worms is most necessary, and saves its cost over and over in sweeping and rolling, besides saving the damage done in sweeping off their casts, and their removal greatly improves the green for putting and in its general appearance. The best time for applying wormkillers is autumn when the greens are wet, and in mild weather when the worms are working freely.

Seeding.

I have been more successful in sowing grass seeds in September than in the spring, and the grass gets a good start before the winter sets in, and gets well rooted before the heat of the following summer. Besides, the birds are more troublesome in spring than autumn, as in autumn there is plenty of other food to be found.

The land for seeding should be treated much the same as for garden seeds, except that the mould need not be worked so deep, but should be mixed with sand. A good plan is to cover the seed with a dressing of mould, then roll down firm. As soon as the grass has grown long enough, it should be mown, but not too closely at first, and the grass left on. Greens that are wanted for immediate use should be turfed: when so treated they become playable almost at once.

Watering.

When greens are dried up, a good watering will revive the grass and greatly improve them for putting by softening the surface, which is likely to be very fast, but they must be thoroughly saturated so as to keep moist for some time. Watering sparingly is worse than not at all, as it scalds the grass and the sun burns worse than before.

The cost of making a nine-hole course in parks is much as follows :—

COURSES IN PARKS

For 9 Approaches,	£15	15	0
„ 2 Levelled Greens,	20	0	0
„ 7 Natural Greens,	28	0	0
„ 9 Tees,	2	5	0
Top Dressing for Greens,	3	7	6
Chemical Manure,	4	0	0
Total, not including Tools,	£73	7	6

Where parks are rough and require clearing, the cost would be more; and, again, in some parks a course could be made at less cost. I have seen some that are fed as short as is required for a course, so that only tees and greens want making. Of the last four holes that I made, three of which had levelled and one a natural green, the cost, including four tees and four approaches, was about £45. I think, as a rough guess, that a nine-hole course could be made in almost any park for from £60 to £150.

Upkeep of a Nine-Hole Course.

In parks where they are close fed, as they should be, one man could keep a nine-hole course, with help to do extras, but where there is a lot of grass and it grows fast, it would require a man and a lad, and perhaps a pony, to do the mowing in a wet season. The cost, with the exception of wages and tools, would be :—

Rolling through the Greens twice a year,	£3	0	0
Chemical Manure (average),	2	0	0
Earth Worm Destroyer,	3	0	0
	£8	0	0

[E. Mepham's experience, detailed in the above chapter, is based mainly on work done in Buckhurst Park in Sussex, in the occupancy of Mr. R. H. Benson, where he has made a park course, and kept it up in a very high state of perfection. It is a course that has various kinds of soil, so that various methods have been tried on the greens. Perhaps the most valuable of his hints are in connection with the sweeping, the necessity that this should not be overdone, especially in winter, and that it should be done across the incline in case of sloping greens; and in connection with the dressing, that this should be varied from one year to another. With regard to the watering, I think that keepers of park courses, as well as others, should take note of the hint elaborated by Mr. Fowler and other writers, to the effect that water is far best applied by a sprinkler, which deposits the water lightly, in drops, like rain.—ED.]

PARK HAZARDS.

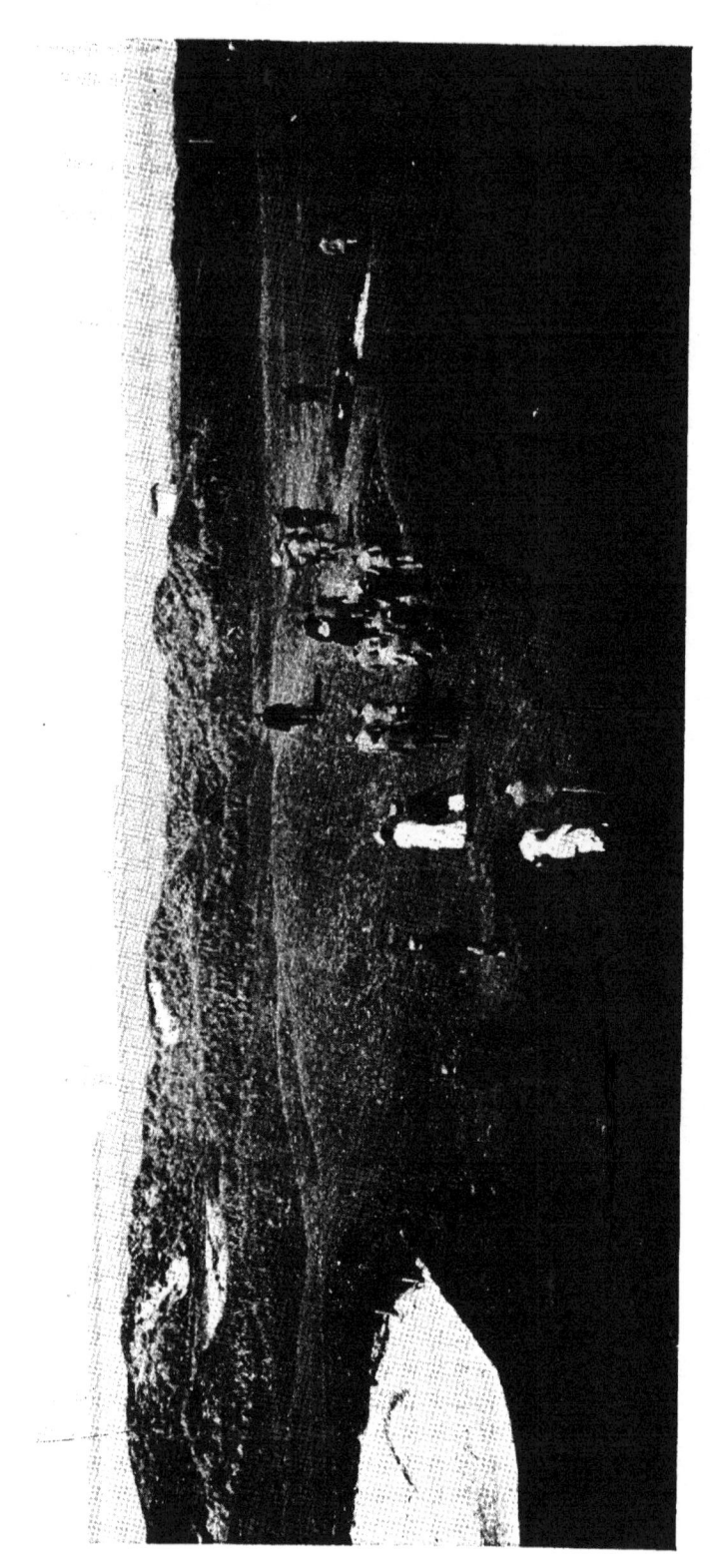

IDEAL LINKS GROUND.

CHAPTER XII

THE FORMATION AND PLACING OF HAZARDS

By Mr. C. K. HUTCHISON (*Coldstream Guards*)

IN the construction of a new course, one of the most difficult questions to decide is the nature and position of the hazards. On the real sea links, where natural hazards abound, the problem of the form and character of the hazard is generally solved for you; but on inland courses, where most of the bunkers have to be constructed, this question becomes a really difficult one. Hazards can be divided into two classes—floral and sand. Of the first variety, which includes gorse, heather, rushes, trees, and rough grass, there is seldom any lack, but to make your course interesting, these existing hazards should be supplemented by some kind of sand bunker. Now, a sand bunker should fulfil two requirements. It should be sufficiently wide and deep to catch and retain bad shots, and the formation should be such as to allow a player a fair chance of regaining the fair-way in one shot. For this reason the faces should be sloped, and not perpendicular. The combination of narrow trench and perpendicular rampart, which you find in so many inland courses, is, in my opinion, the worst class of hazard. The bad shot constantly escapes by jumping over it, and the ball which just fails to carry, and strikes the top of the bank, falls back under the face, affording but little chance of recovery.

These bunkers, which have been humourously termed potato-pits, disfigure many otherwise excellent courses, and the mere sight of the ramparts is quite sufficient to prejudice the majority of players against any course possessing them. Even on some of the famous sea links, the formation and position of some of the hazards leave considerable room for improvement.

As regards formation, Muirfield is, perhaps, the worst offender. Nearly every bunker on this course has an absolutely perpendicular face, thus introducing a great element of chance as to the punishment a bad shot receives. This is more especially the case because, unless you have the misfortune to be under the face, your ball will generally be lying quite clear. The bunker guarding the eighteenth green is a wretched type of hazard, consisting, as it does, of a deep, narrow, trench-like bunker, with perpendicular sides, which a bad shot often jumps, and in which you may find your ball practically unplayable. A good recovery from a bunker, especially when that bunker is close to the green, is one of the most satisfactory strokes in the game, and it demands great skill and experience in the execution. It seems a great pity that hazards should be made of this unplayable nature, thus reducing every player to the same level. Gorse, for this reason, is an unsatisfactory hazard. Unless you can lift and drop, under a local rule, it is long odds on your ball being impossible to play. Some of the bunkers at Walton Heath—I refer to those without any accompanying rampart—are excellent examples of a good artificial hazard. They invariably catch a bad shot, and anyone versed in the art of bunker play should be able to get out in one stroke. Fairly wide, fairly deep, and with sloping sides, they fulfil the conditions of the ideal artificial bunker.

A bunker should be made deep enough to avoid the necessity of having an accompanying mound. These mounds not only disfigure the links, but often prevent the bottom of the pin being seen when approaching the hole, thereby turning the hole into a semi-blind one.

Having decided on the formation of your hazard, the still more difficult question of position has to be considered. Firstly, with regard to the tee shot, some kind of punishment should always await the topped shot. Rough grass, heather, or rushes for upwards of a hundred yards in front of the tee, provide the best kind of hazard to meet the case. Bunkers, when possible, should be placed so that the surrounding ground " draws " towards them. This is one of the characteristics of the St. Andrews hazards, and it makes them trebly difficult to avoid. I am certainly not an advocate of having a long carry to negotiate at every tee. It becomes wearisome, and with adverse winds impracticable. It affords far better sport to tempt a man to risk a long carry to gain a distinct advantage, leaving him an alternative route, than to compel him to attempt shots that he considers to be beyond his powers. For this reason, the tee shots to the seventeenth hole at St. Andrews, the sixth hole at Muirfield, and the third hole at Sandwich are three of the best I know. By bringing off the bold shot in each case you gain a considerable advantage, while there is a safer alternative route in each case. Another interesting tee shot is afforded by a hazard which forms an angle past which you must steer your ball, making a kind of "round-the-corner" hole. There should be plenty of safe ground to the side, but the man who can just slip past the hazard should gain a material advantage over his fainter-hearted opponent who has steered a wider and less perilous course.

These so-called "pinching shots" afford great satisfaction when successfully negotiated, and test not only a player's powers but also his self-confidence. This kind of hole is unfortunately seldom to be met with on inland courses, where, as a rule, you have to drive straight down a fair-way bounded by parallel lines of heather

SYLVAN HAZARDS.

FLORAL HAZARDS.

FORMATION AND PLACING OF HAZARDS 159

or whins. This, undoubtedly, becomes very monotonous, and seems unnecessary, when, by a little zig-zagging, by leaving corners of rough grass or whins jutting out into the course, or by means of a judiciously-placed bunker, you could make the kind of hole I have attempted to describe. There are several excellent holes of this type at Huntercombe, and the eighth hole at Woking and the fourteenth hole at Byfleet afford good instances. But the hazard, which controls the playing of this species of hole, must, to my mind, be plainly visible from the tee. Hidden pots in the centre of the course cannot surely be deemed fair hazards. But if the same bunker is plainly visible from the tee, it is your business to avoid it however near the line of play it may be, and you will only have yourself to blame if you find your ball trapped. If your course is somewhat narrow, and is bounded by rough grass or heather, it is a good plan to keep about ten yards on each side cut moderately short, so that the ball which is just off the course may not meet with such severe punishment as the wild, boomerang shot, which richly deserves its fate. Trees do not generally afford a good golfing hazard, but if their presence on the course is inevitable, the ground under them should be kept cleared : otherwise they will be responsible for much tedious ball-hunting.

The question of the relative position of hazards to putting greens has given rise to much controversy amongst players, and there has always been a considerable diversity of opinion on this point. There are some people who affirm that a hole is not properly guarded unless there is a hazard stretching right across the course immediately in front of the putting green. Others vigorously protest against this class of hazard, insisting that there should always be a clear run up to the hole, and that the bunkers should be to the side of the green. The relative position of hazard to putting green must depend so much on the length of the hole and formation of the ground that it is impossible to lay down any rules. What you really want are hazards so placed as to compel the player to use a variety of shots. A series of pitching shots becomes monotonous, and too many running-up approaches are equally tiresome. What you want is variety, and in this respect North Berwick always appeals to me more than any other course I have played over. On the majority of courses, especially in the South, hazards are placed too far away from the holes they are intended to guard. At St. Andrews the bunkers are close in at the side of the holes, and when a competition is in progress many of the holes are actually placed within three or four yards of the hazard. Many of the holes at North Berwick are in similar proximity to the hazards. The approach play, as a result, is full of interest, and affords a splendid test of accuracy and confidence in what

FORMATION AND PLACING OF HAZARDS 161

is generally considered to be the most scientific part of the game. These remarks especially apply to the shorter holes. The shorter the approach shot the more difficult that shot should be made. The hole which requires two full shots to reach it need not be so carefully guarded as the drive-and-iron, or one-shot, hole. The mere length of the former calls for accurate hitting if the green is to be reached in the proper number of strokes. The short holes that can be reached from the tee should be bristling with hazards, demanding a perfect shot to be played in order to reach the green. "The Redan" at North Berwick and the eleventh hole at St. Andrews are two magnificent examples, and all the short holes at Walton Heath are excellent. In the two-shot holes, requiring a brassey or cleck for the second shot, let there be a hazard to carry with the second shot by all means, but do not place that hazard too near to the hole. With a following wind it becomes impossible to carry the hazard and stay on the green. There are several holes of this description at Sandwich, which, to my mind, are spoilt by the cross hazard being placed too close to the hole. For instance, with a following wind it is hardly possible to stay on the first, thirteenth, fourteenth, and fifteenth greens however perfectly you have played your second shot. This state of things is surely wrong. Bunkers should be placed to punish indifferent shots, not to prevent the playing of good ones. The latest courses, such as Walton Heath, Huntercombe, and Sunningdale, show a very marked improvement in this respect, and, though not very well known, Northwood is hard to beat for position and formation of the hazards, and is certainly one of the most interesting inland courses I have played over. In conclusion, there is one piece of advice I have to offer to those who find themselves responsible for the construction of a new course: do not be in a hurry to make bunkers. If you do, you are pretty certain to find that many of them are in entirely wrong places, the result being useless expenditure of time and money. Hazards are the finishing touches which make or mar a course, and such a weighty matter cannot be too carefully considered.

CHAPTER XIII

REMARKS ON THE LAYING OUT OF COURSES

By H. H. Hilton

To make, just a slight explanation at the beginning of this chapter, I would remark that I do not for a moment pose as an expert in the laying out of a golf course, and much less do I wish to place myself upon the pedestal which denotes the position of an authority on the maintenance and upkeep of a green. But during the past fifteen years I have had more than an average experience of golf courses, their laying out and the upkeep thereof; and during this time I think I have turned this experience to advantage, as I have always tried to sit at the feet of those who, through the necessity of long and varied experience, must have gained a thorough and comprehensive knowledge of their subjects, and in sitting at their feet a certain amount of wisdom is sure to be imbibed.

Laying Out a Course.

Given virgin ground, it is, I think, always wise, first of all, to take a thorough survey of the natural formation of the said ground, for unless you do so it is impossible to arrive at a more or less methodical plan of campaign, and it is very essential that the man who attempts to lay out a course should have in his head more than a mere general knowledge of the ground at command before he commences to map out the position where the putting greens should be. If he selects these spots in a species of haphazard manner, he is apt to find himself in a hopeless muddle before he has arranged for the position of two-thirds of the necessary number of holes. It is no use proceeding forth to pick out suitable sites for putting greens, caring not how and from where these putting greens have to be approached. This savours too much of the enthusiastic individual who selects pretty spots for pic-nic luncheons. Pic-nics are but things of a day, but a putting green on a golf links is a fixture for many years to come—at least it should be so, unless money is of no object and the wild and indiscriminate laying down of putting greens can be well afforded. Many a time have I seen money simply thrown to the winds through the too enthusiastic appreciation of a particularly suitable site for a putting green. The green has been laid almost irrespective of the question whether or not it is possible to make it fit in with the general map of the course. It is the old, old story : marry in haste and repent at leisure ; and many a custodian of club finance has had occasion to rue the impetuosity of some leading member of committee who, infatuated with the importance of his own "find," has persisted in having the work completed at once. It is the members who have to pay the piper: all that the author of the unnecessary expense has to bear is the stigma that he is responsible for it; but a conscience is not given to everyone. These monuments to impetuosity are to be seen studded all over the links in the kingdom, particularly those of a seaside description, and the wondering stranger looks at them and, pondering, remarks, "What is that supposed to be?" "Oh, that is 'James's folly.'" "What is 'James's folly'?" "Oh, he thought he would like a green there, and he had one." "Whatever for?" "Please do not ask me. Kindly ask James: he is the only one who ever did know."

Still, notwithstanding these occasional lapses from sanity, it is well when commencing to lay out a course to fix upon one or two spots on the ground which particularly lend themselves to the formation of putting greens, not only owing to the natural adaptation of the ground for the greens, but also on account of the natural hazards which surround the greens, as natural hazards are invariably to be preferred to artificial ones, even if only on the question of expense. Such ideal situations are to be found on nearly every tract of land, and in picking them out and marking them down in the memory they are exceedingly useful for further reference, as you are thereby able to work to and from these particular landmarks. Of course, it may happen that one or other of these landmarks may eventually have to be given up, but this cannot be helped, as you must not sacrifice the general run of a course for one individual hole however good that hole may be. Only a short time ago I was discussing this subject with a man who has made more than a qualified success in the laying out of a course in close vicinity to the metropolis, and I happened to remark that I always considered it advisable, first of all, to pick out the positions most suitable for the short holes, and then to try and work from those positions. " It is just what I did," he remarked. " I first marked out the short sixth hole, and worked from it "; and this opinion certainly tended to endorse the strength of my view on the wisdom of this method.

Of course, this plan of procedure is only applicable when the links architect has literally virgin ground at command—that is to say, the species of ground on which there are no great obstructions, such as the ground on which a course like Walton Heath has been laid out, or one might even include Sunningdale, although it is very evident in the case of the latter that a goodly number of pine trees had to be sacrificed in order to complete some of the holes, notably the seventh, which has apparently been literally

LAYING OUT COURSES

carved right through the wood. But Sunningdale was laid out almost irrespective of cost, and one could almost say that the links architect had a free hand. Whether he made the most of his opportunities is a question which I have often heard discussed, and there are people closely associated with and keenly interested in the club who look not upon these discussions in a friendly spirit. But even Paradise might be improved, and, good as are the links at Walton Heath, Sunningdale, and Huntercombe, it is more than probable that there are people in this world who might by chance make happy suggestions—suggestions which in the end would benefit the course, as a test of the game—and to make a links a good test is surely the main object in laying it out. There are people, however, who, with a view to the artistic, have the most rooted objection to anything being removed; and, speaking of inland courses, there must be numberless trees on the golf links in the kingdom which are quite unfair hazards. Possibly they are very fine trees, and from a scenic point of view it would seem a pity to sacrifice them in the cause of the goddess of golf, but a golf course is a golf course, and these sacrifices have to be made for the sake of the game. And it is in this respect that the majority of the members of Green Committees show such a lack of judgment, and one might even go further, and say lack of common sense. There is a hazard on their course—say, for argument's sake, it is a tree. Literally every stranger who plays on the links condemns this hazard as unfair, and condemns it in no half-hearted manner. Will the Green Committee listen to the voice of the stranger? Not they. Their manner suggests that it is bordering on the precincts of an insult that the question should even be discussed—at least discussed in a derogatory light. Eventually that hazard is removed, but it is only removed many years after it has been freely discussed and also freely condemned. The committee have at last hauled down their flag to the continuous bombardment, but they invariably take what may be termed a *stupid*, obstinate pride in the fact that they have held out so long. The voice of the stranger—at least the stranger who has had any experience of the game—is always worth listening to. He appears on the links with an open mind; his mind is not warped with the prejudices of many years' association. He may suggest alterations which are not possible, or he may suggest alterations which are palpably not advisable, but his words are always worth consideration and worth weighing up. A man who plays on a links day after day is more than apt to pass over any little defects in the course. He gradually becomes acclimatised to these failings, and it is only the kindly, critical stranger who can point these failings out. In doing so, he is only doing a kindly service to the club. He is unconsciously the "Good Samaritan." As I have said before, he may suggest many things which are inadvisable, but if he suggests even one thing which is advisable, his criticism is not in vain.

When laying out a course there is an old saying which may always be followed, and that is, "Two heads are always better than one." A man may be the greatest living expert in this branch of the golfing profession, but however great his knowledge may be, and however thoroughly he may have thought out his subject and his plan of campaign, it is always possible for someone to make a happy suggestion which would be of material advantage. The fable tells us that the mouse once helped the lion out of a serious difficulty, and in the laying out of a course the golfing mouse may, by a happy inspiration, often keep the golfing lion out of an awkward dilemma. I remember once being asked to help a committee out of one of these trying situations. Two men who knew the ground thoroughly had been trying to work out a problem. It was one of those problems where a course had to be extended, the extra ground at command being limited and not of the finest quality, and the object of the committee was to secure as much length as was permissible, and at the same time retain as many of the features of the old course as possible. It was not difficult to lay out seventeen good holes, but no one could say where the eighteenth was to come from, and two days' solemn consideration brought us no nearer the

M

solution. Eventually a full committee meeting was called, in the hope that some member or other thereof could find some happy inspiration. The happy inspiration did come, and, extraordinary to say, it came from a man who was only on the committee from the point of mere courtesy, as he was a man with a handicap of 30, played about once each year, and knew about as much about golf as a doorpost. But the golfing mouse had saved the situation. Before that conclave was over, however, the mouse afterwards unfortunately attempted the feat of transforming himself into a lion, as he wanted to alter the whole course from beginning to end. But the committee came to the conclusion that one happy inspiration was sufficient for the day thereof—at least in his case.

"Marry in haste and repent at leisure": cut your bunkers in haste and fill them up at leisure. This is very true, as there are so many individuals who, in their enthusiasm, wish a course to be completed in a week, and in consequence make hazards all over the course: hazards which at the time may be quite fair, but as the nature of the turf changes, as it always does with continuous rolling and cutting, these hazards are found to be in ridiculous positions. I know of a course in the North of England on which a great deal of money was wasted in this way. The committee were solemnly warned by more than one authority that it was not advisable to cut the bunkers out until they found by experience where they should be placed; and, again, it was pointed out that the nature of the turf was sure to alter, and that in the course of six months or so the balls would be running much farther than they were at the time of the opening of the links. They saw the wisdom of this suggestion, but the members began to clamour for more hazards, and the committee eventually gave way, and gave them these hazards, and a goodly number of them too, with the result that within the next two years a good half of them had to be filled up again—and filling up a bunker is just about as expensive as cutting one, particularly when the soil or sand for filling in has to be carted from a considerable distance. Rome was not built in a day, and you cannot build a golf course in a day.

CHAPTER XIV

THE CHAPTERSHIP COURSES

By H. H. HILTON.

Introductory.

"A CHAMPIONSHIP course" is a vague and evasive term, as it is capable of more than one interpretation. There are a few who have settled ideas of the interpretation of the term, and that is that "a Championship course" is a links which should embody every available natural attribute, and represent absolutely the very truest and, at the same time, the very severest test of the game, but such tracts of land are not to be found, and even the hand of man cannot fashion them in such a complete form as to thoroughly conform to this high notion, and in consequence the ideal Championship course is still in embryo. It is said that our friends in the land of many dollars have in contemplation the construction of a course in which will be embodied the main features of many of the finest holes to be found on links in the British Isles, but it is more than probable that it will be found that this is a task which is beyond even the limits of illimitable dollars,

SAND BUNKERS AT MUIRFIELD.

SAND BUNKER AT HUNSTANTON.

as whilst nature may be copied the imitation must have upon it the finger prints of artificiality.

There are five courses on which the Championship is at present played, and if every critic had his will, there would not be a single course of these five on which the Championship would again be played. And, again, if every critic had his will there would be many other courses in the kingdom on which the Championship would be played at varying periods. How many links have at one time or another been mentioned to me as worthy of the honour of a Championship being played upon them? I should not like to count, but in the majority of cases the suggestion is somewhat easily dismissed, as there is always the simple query, "No doubt a very fine links, but where would the people stay?" "Well, perhaps that *is* a difficulty," comes the reply, and that is undoubtedly a very grave difficulty and one not easily overcome.

"Why are the Championships always played over these same five links?" is a question which is very often asked, and it is a very easy question to answer, as they are the links over which certain five influential clubs hold sway. In fact, these five clubs literally manage the Championship contests, and it cannot be gainsaid that they nowadays manage these little affairs with more than an average degree of success. How it came about that these said five clubs came to hold this supreme power is another question, and one which would take a great deal of space to explain, and, notwithstanding the many suggestions as to the advisability of breaking up this close corporation and taking one or other of the championships to fields and pastures new, I can hardly think that there is the slightest possibility of such an event happening, and the good people of Westward Ho will yet have to sigh awhile, and our friends from the Emerald Isle will certainly have reason to produce stronger arguments than they have at command at present to prevail upon the powers that be to flit across the water in the month of May.

Section I.—St. Andrews.

Now, I am told that it is actual heresy to even murmur a suggestion that the classic green of St. Andrews is not all that it should be as a test of the game, but, heresy or no heresy, I cannot help thinking that it is just a little bit open to criticism, chiefly on account of the fact that to a stranger, or even a comparative stranger, it is quite impossible exactly to locate the numerous bunkers which are invisible from the teeing ground. When lately discussing this question with a well-known critic, who has an absorbing affection for the classic green, I was plainly told that a man who could not learn the locality of the bunkers at St. Andrews in the course of two or three days had no right to call himself a golfer, I could not help remarking, "Surely you mean two or three years." I suppose the suggestion was ill advised; all I know is that I quickly found myself in disgrace, and remained more or less so to the end of the meeting. But I found quite a humorous side to the situation, as I persisted in following up the argument, and made many suggestions which bordered on the verge of sacrilege. Eventually the discussion came to an end, as my worthy friend, for whose opinion in other matters regarding the game of golf I have the greatest respect, somewhat tardily came to the conclusion that some of my suggestions were not made in quite the best of faith. And his diagnosis of the case was quite correct: I was simply amusing myself at his expense, and he eventually found me out.

Now, St. Andrews must be a very fine test of the game: so many people say so: in fact a great number hold decided opinions that it is the one great test of the game in the kingdom. But I hold an opinion that a great many of these would-be devotees of the classic green are not exactly voicing their own personal opinion, possibly for the reason that their insufficiency of knowledge does not enable them to arrive at a just conclusion as to what a golf links should be in order to supply a test of golf. So they voice the opinion of others: the voice of men who are qualified by their knowledge and experience to hold views which are worthy of respect. Again, there are others who say, " Oh, there is no test like St.

Andrews!" and in saying it are simply uttering, parrot-like, the cry of fashion, as it is fashionable to express the opinion that St. Andrews is the one and only test of the game; it hall-marks a man as a judge of the game to say this—at least the man himself thinks so.

But on the principle that there is never smoke without fire, it must be true that the classic green does provide a good test of a player's golfing ability. Firstly, that it calls for a wonderful variety of strokes, admits of no doubt. You can invariably run your approaches if you please; or, again, if you wish it, you can play the half-pitch-and-run approach. It is a most telling shot—in fact, it is the one stroke in the repertoire of a golfer which is essential at St. Andrews. There are very many opportunities granted of employing the aid of this shot, and there are few men who have learned their game at St. Andrews who are not more or less experts in this class of stroke. Again, you can always attempt to pitch an approach shot at St. Andrews. I advisedly say *attempt*, as from my own experience, and the experience gained in the rôle of an interested and critical spectator, I have come to the conclusion that it is a shot which should be avoided at St. Andrews as much as possible: there are so many banks and braes just in front of the green that one often courts disaster by pitching the ball high up in the air. There are very few greens indeed on which even

Taylor, with all the underspin he gets on the ball, can rely on remaining near the hole with a pitched-up shot; and Taylor has found this out to his cost in the past. In fact, when playing St. Andrews—at least when playing St. Andrews when the turf is not on the heavy side—it is always advisable to avoid the high-lofted approach, and in this, I think, lies a certain weakness in the conformation of the course. The St. Andrews golfer is so seldom called upon to play a lofted approach on his own course that when he wanders abroad he is very much at sea when he is called upon to play such a shot; and this was very evident at Prestwick, in 1905, when Mr. Gordon Barry made many very scratchy efforts to play the delicate pitching approaches which one is often called upon to play on the West of Scotland green. But this lack of confidence when playing high-lofted approaches is a feature of the majority of golfers who have learned their game at St. Andrews, and I have noticed that the majority of them invariably play the stroke with an exceptionally lofted club, invariably a sign of want of confidence. Again, the St. Andrews man is apt to be a wild driver. This is easily understood, as it is a green on which there is either very little room or, on the other hand, a great deal. By this I mean you have either to keep desperately straight or else very, very crooked: if you wander away just a little bit from the straight and narrow pathway you are often badly trapped, but a riotous, herculean blow, such as Mr. "Ted" Blackwell often hits, lands up on some unheard-of place, but lands quite safe and sound. I do not suppose any player enjoys himself quite as much over St. Andrews as does this mighty swiper. The bunkers were not fashioned for such as he: he treats them with contempt. But there is one great charm about St. Andrews, and that is that you can play it in so many ways. Mr. Blackwell plays it in one way—a way not given to every golfer. The short driver can employ other methods, and often, as in the case of the hare and the tortoise, the tortoise reaches the post first; but the difficulty for the stranger is to arrive at the happy medium. His mind is torn with doubt from beginning to end of the week's play. Personally, I hold the opinion that, when in doubt, to play safe is the correct method. I know this method paid me well in the Championship in 1901.

There is one shot which the classic green has successfully taught its many pupils, and that is the forcing wrist iron-shot: the long approach shot, which keeps low, pitches half way, and runs the rest. Mr. James Robb played this shot to perfection at Hoylake, and with the rubber-cored ball there is no other shot quite as telling.

Section II.—*Muirfield.*

Muirfield is generally accredited with the

character of being *the one* of the five Championship courses which cannot quite claim on merit alone to be altogether worthy of the honour conferred upon it. The fact is, Muirfield was thrust upon the golfing world as a Championship course, and thrust for the reason that the Honourable Company of Edinburgh Golfers is one of the five clubs governing the Open Championship, and when its members decided to remove their golfing habitation from Musselburgh they settled their minds upon this walled-in enclosure near Drem, and the Championship had to be played there whether the golfing world wanted to or not. The good people of Musselburgh were amongst those who did not want it to be played at Muirfield, for the sufficient reason that it was taking the Championship meeting away from their own links. Their protest resolved itself into the holding of an open meeting just prior to the meeting at Muirfield, and some fondly hoped that this meeting would be looked upon as the real Championship meeting. The entry was an excellent one, as nearly every professional of note competed—and wisely too, as the prize money was lavish, and it is a professional's business to earn money by the playing of the game of golf—but I hardly think that anyone, aside and apart from those who had reason to take a vivid interest in the Musselburgh course, ever considered that there was any possibility of this opposition show being considered the real Championship contest.

Whether Musselburgh at the time was a better test of the game than the *initial* course at Muirfield is a question best left to those who were thoroughly acquainted with both links, but if Musselburgh did not provide a better test than the course over which the Championship was played in 1892, all I can say is that the Championship never should have been played over Musselburgh, as when one looks back and reflects, it is more and more driven home to one what a shockingly indifferent course it was. It lacked length, it moreover lacked condition, and altogether there were about four good holes on it. In later years someone set to work and attempted a metamorphosis at Muirfield, and the man who did it accomplished wonders. He got more out of the ground than ever appeared possible, and as a feat of golf links architecture it stands unrivalled, as, in the first instance, he obtained length, and that was very difficult in such a confined space, and moreover he managed to eliminate several indifferent holes. That was not so difficult on account of the fact that he had so much material to work upon. And, again, he considerably improved many of the holes. In fact he accomplished just about all that was possible for a human being to do; and still there is a doubt whether Muirfield is quite a sufficiently good course to merit the distinction of a Championship being played over it. The truth is, nature has not been sufficiently kind to allow a first-class course

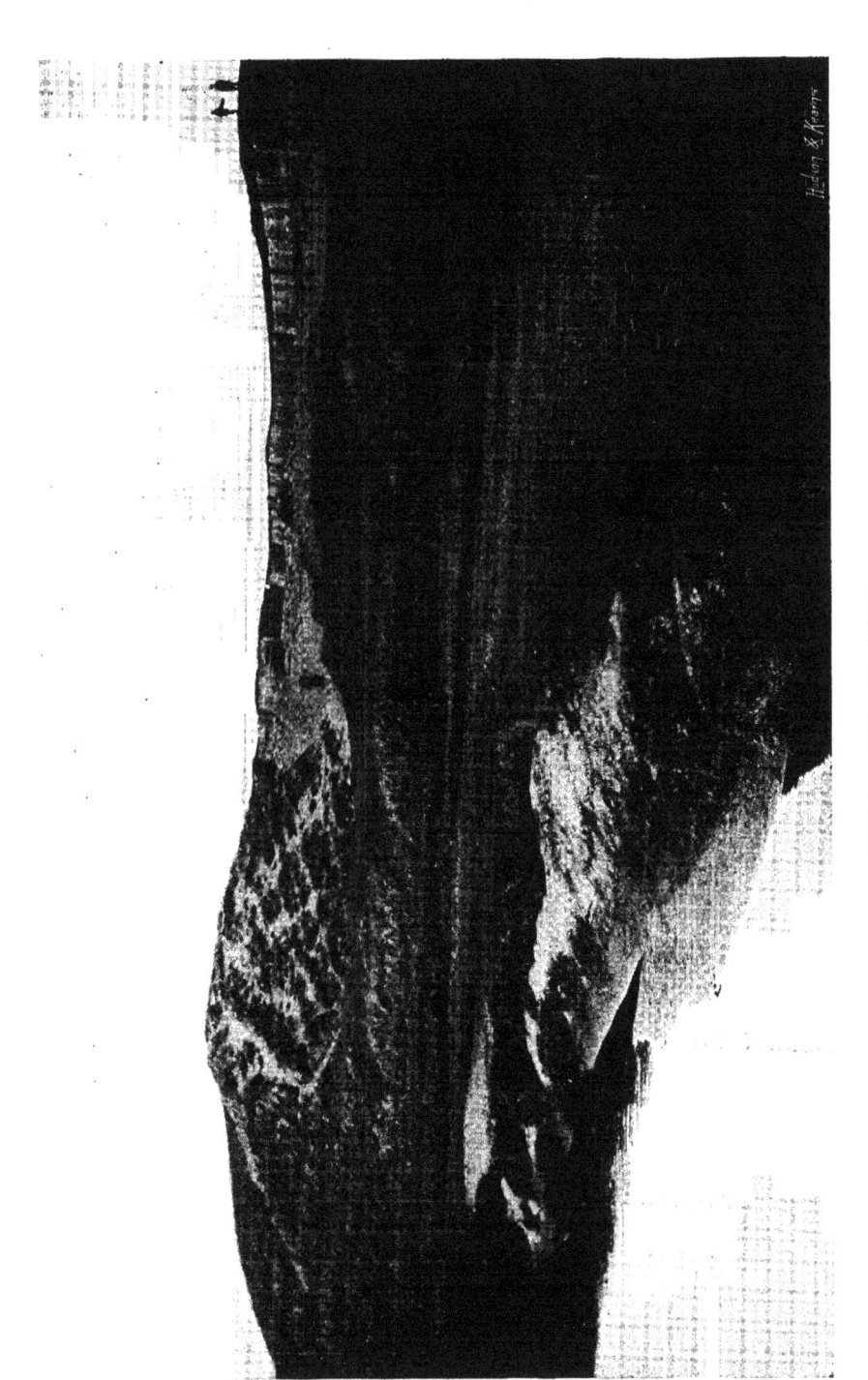

SAND AND WATER.

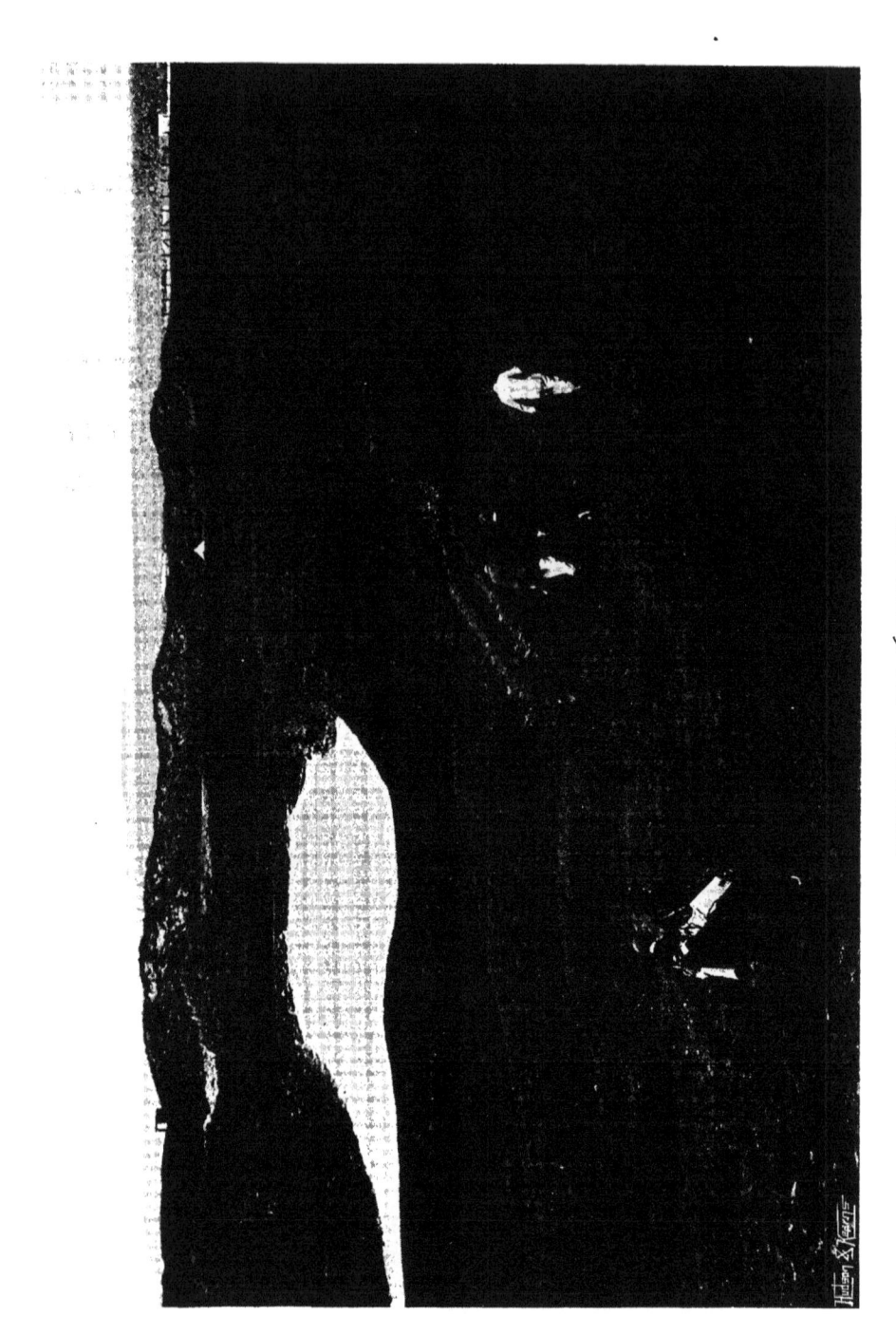

BUNKERS EN ÉCHELON.

to be built in the space at command, and, again, the hand of man has built a wall round the links, and that wall is neither fair as a hazard nor is it picturesque in appearance. There are good holes at Muirfield, and a goodly number of them, as, for instance, the second, the twelfth, and the eighteenth, all, peculiar to say, of a somewhat similar character, but there are few holes that are really interesting at Muirfield. No doubt every man when he is playing an important medal round finds in his mind sufficient anxiety to make every hole interesting, but it is a very different matter to judge a course in cold blood, and you can only arrive at an equitable conclusion by watching others play the course. The main hazard at Muirfield, which is undoubtedly the rough grass on either side of the course, does not always mete out just punishment to the wandering player, as, whilst it is often possible to obtain a very bad lie therein, on the other hand many a very wild stroke goes literally unpunished. It is a peculiar kind of "rough," as the grass grows in tufts, and seems to be intersected by numerous narrow pathways, and the lies in these pathways are invariably good, but if you do happen to find a tuft of grass just behind your ball, much better would it be for you that your ball had found a sand hazard. Muirfield has two great qualifications, one being that the teeing grounds are good, and the other that the putting greens are, on the whole, very fair. One or two, notably the second, third, and twelfth, are a little apt to become too keen, and in consequence tricky, but, on the whole, the putting is fair, and, moreover, not as easy as it looks, as there are numberless minute hummocks on many of the greens, which cause trouble to the careless putter who will not take the trouble to find out the correct line to the hole.

Section III.—Hoylake.

Hoylake is a course which from time to time has had many stones thrown at it, and Hoylake is a course which probably deserves just a few of these missiles. It is flat and comparatively uninteresting, says the man who has been in the habit of playing over Prestwick, Sandwich, and other links of a similar character. Well, in its main features it has a flat appearance, as there are no hazards of the magnitude of "The Maiden" at Sandwich or "The Himalayas" at Prestwick to be found on the Cheshire green; but I hardly think it just to term Hoylake uninteresting. Let anyone play the course in a west wind, even if that wind be of moderate strength, and he will find a good deal of interest, and a good deal of thinking required as to how he is to play his shots. Ask Robb and Lingen whether they found the course uninteresting in the final of the last Championship. Certainly they had to contend against a really strong west wind; but it is a west wind which brings out the true value of the Hoylake course. With the wind blowing from the east, the course is infinitely easier. Now, as regards this reputation for flatness, as I have said before, the general contour of the ground is certainly flat, but on close inspection it will be found that the surface of the ground is one mass of small undulations, and seldom do you obtain an absolutely ideal stance. When playing a shot through the green at Hoylake (and in this the course bears a strict resemblance to St. Andrews), it is these unequal stances which bring out the true ability of the golfer. It is not at all difficult to hit a ball when the stance is what may be termed plumb and the lie a good one : this is the A B C of golf ; but it is a very different thing to hit a ball when it is lying at an awkward angle and you have to take your stance with one foot placed inches above the other. The playing of such a shot requires a good deal of the knowledge of the game and the correct application thereof. During the past year I have had to play a good deal on inland courses, and I have come to the conclusion that playing through the green on inland courses is infinitely easier than on seaside courses. Certainly the stances one obtains on inland courses are not always exactly what one would ask for, but they are infinitely easier than those to be found on seaside courses ; and it was coming back to Hoylake after a year's practice on inland greens that brought home to my mind the minor inequalities in the ground at Hoylake. I found that I had to stand in awkward positions, which worried me considerably. I had really never noticed them before; no doubt I had become acclimatised to them through years of familiar association; but they are there, and I have come to the conclusion that Hoylake supplies anything but billiard-table golf.

It is infinitely easier to form an opinion of a course when you have been away from it for some time. If you play on it day by day you are apt to shut your eyes to its defects, and just take it as it is. It is to the stranger that you have to trust to point out its defects. Now, I came back to Hoylake after an absence of fourteen months, and the first thing that struck me was that it was an ugly-looking course, with its numerous turf banks and hazards right across the links. There is a species of inland artificiality about it which is not pleasing to the eye. Not that this in the slightest degree affects the links as a test of the game. On this point I have only one opinion, and that is that it provides an excellent test, partly for the reason that there is any amount of length, and a man has to play with his head, and partly because it is a course on which many risks may be taken, provided the player feels inclined to do so. But there are far too many hazards stretched right across the course. For instance, take the bunker which stretches across the course about 220 yards from the third tee. In the first

GOOD TEE SHOT BUNKER.

ALPS GREEN—HOYLAKE.

days of the Championship week literally every player had to play short either with an iron club or a spoon, and, again, had to spare his second shot. It was making a farce of what might be made a good hole. True it is that the wind was blowing from a somewhat unusual quarter, but it blows sufficiently often from an easterly direction to warrant the belief that it would improve the hole if the centre of the hazard was filled up so as to allow the long smiters occasionally to have a go to get home in two. Even as it stands, Mr. Blackwell scorned this selfsame hazard, and against Mr. Orr was home in two; but there are very few "Ted" Blackwells in the world of golf.

Again, the next hole, "The Cop," is far from an ideal one. It is a hole which is a very old institution at Hoylake, and it savours of vandalism to interfere with a hole which has stood as it is for over thirty years. But in these thirty years times have changed, the most important change of all being the introduction of the rubber-cored ball, and that has affected nearly every course in the kingdom. This hole against a west wind could hardly be improved upon, but during the Championship week the wind decided to blow from the other quarter, and the bunker being so near the hole, it was only the slightly-missed shot—that shot which a player unintentionally gets a little bit under—which could possibly remain near the hole, and that is not as it should be. If that cross bunker was taken away in the centre, and a few more hazards introduced round the green, "The Cop" hole at Hoylake might be made worthy of the name of a good short hole. But this is not the only case at Hoylake where advisable alterations could be made, as whilst the cross bunkers running right across the course are essential in a few cases to add variety to the links, still, they are gradually becoming a thing of the past, and the intelligent men who lay out golf courses are gradually reducing them to a comparative minimum. They are meeting the requirements of the rubber-cored ball, and the correct and most artistic shot with the rubber-cored ball is what is termed the half-pitch-and-run.

By the way, it has always struck me as somewhat peculiar that nearly all the golfers who commenced their golfing education at Hoylake originally played all their approaches with lofting irons. Now Hoylake is at present essentially a course on which the running shot pays. I can remember the days when we looked upon the man who ran his ball up to the hole, particularly if he ran it up with a wooden putter, as a species of cowardly funk, but I have since learned that it is the safer shot of the two. One can always imbibe wisdom, even at an advanced age. It is difficult to explain why they cultivate this shot, as Hoylake has always been a course on which it was possible to play a large number of running approaches. Possibly the youth of Hoylake

WELL GUARDED GREEN.

AMPHITHEATRE GREEN.

instinctively copied some of the celebrities of old, and I have no doubt that the prowess of Johnnie Ball in this particular stroke had much to do with its cultivation amongst the juniors.

Section IV.—Sandwich.

Sandwich on first appearances is a deceptive-looking course. The varying hazards which can be seen from the first tee, such as " The Maiden," are a little awe-inspiring. They suggest terrible possibilities of disaster, but their bark is distinctly worse than their bite. For anyone who can hit a ball at all far and at all true there is no necessity to get into the embraces of " The Maiden," as, except when there is a really strong head-wind, the carry is of the simplest description. I have seen occasions when, unless there has been a lull in the wind, it is almost impossible to reach the green, but these occasions are few and far between, and the introduction of the rubber-cored ball has very much simplified the dangers and terrors of this notorious hazard: in truth, to anything approaching a good player it is a very simple one-shot hole. But that is a sample of Sandwich from beginning to end: it is a course which appears difficult but which in reality is easy. I am not going to say, as many do, that it is simply a one-shot course and that that shot is the wooden-club shot, as this is not doing justice to the links; but there can be but little doubt that a clean-hit tee shot means much at Sandwich, simply for the reason that it makes the rest of the game easy—and surely that is at it ought to be, as accurate driving is an essential part of the game. That, once having hit your tee shot accurately, there is less to do afterwards at Sandwich than at, say, St. Andrews or Hoylake, admits of no doubt. It is not a green which calls for the same varying and delicate manipulation of the iron clubs that the other two courses do, and, again, the distances are infinitely more easy to judge, but I know no course which repays straight, accurate golf as much as Sandwich does. The really bad shot is invariably badly punished at Sandwich, and the same cannot be said of all the four other Championship courses.

Critics say that Sandwich is so easy, and in this contention they have argument on their side, in that Taylor handed in a card of 68 at the Open Championship meeting, and others have been round under 70. But in what way is it easy? Partly, I contend, on account of the excellent lies you obtain through the green, but chiefly on account of the trueness of the putting greens. Of all the Championship courses the short approaching and putting at Sandwich are infinitely easier than on any of the four other greens, simply for the reason that there is such an even texture of grass upon them that it is easy to gauge the strength of the stroke. At Sandwich a putt of, say, six yards is a simple affair. In playing such a putt the possibility of not laying the ball dead should never enter the mind of a good putter: it should be merely a question as to whether the ball should be holed or not. That is the main reason why White, Braid, and Taylor returned those wonderful scores in 1904: they must have putted well; and, again, they must have driven accurately, as, to my mind, Sandwich is the finest test of accurate driving to be found in the kingdom. At St. Andrews or Hoylake you can afford to founder a goodly number of tee shots. You may, particularly, play that class of shot which comes round with a boomerang-like swing and then runs like a hare. But try that class of shot at Sandwich, and find where you are! You will probably only try it once. If Sandwich has a fault, the fault lies in the fact that it is a course on which you can dispense with the pitch-and-run shot, as you can pitch nearly every approach, particularly when the greens are on the heavy side, and, in consequence, a man who is continually playing over Sandwich is apt to be placed at a serious disadvantage when he is called upon to play upon a course which requires a greater variety of iron play. He must, naturally, find himself in a dilemma. But Sandwich is a good test of the game of golf, and if I were placed in the position of having to back Braid, Taylor, or Vardon against a man whom I thought he would beat, provided the conditions of knowledge of the course were equal, I should have no hesitation in electing Sandwich as a green which provided these conditions.

Section V.—Prestwick.

Prestwick is a course I have always had an affection for—not that I am going to say that it necessarily provides a finer test of the game than any of the four other links over which the Championship is played, but there is so much that is interesting in it. In nearly every tee shot there is an object—you have to keep either to one or other side of the course; or, if this is not necessary, you find it pays to hit a very long ball, and so make for home. The very first hole provides an index as to what is required at Prestwick. It is in some ways an apparently simple tee shot, as there is any amount of room immediately in front of the tee, but the difficulty lies in the fact that the farther your ball travels the greater are the dangers, and, except when you are playing against a strong wind, it is a very open question whether you should play a safe shot or, on the other hand, have a "go" for a long one. If you follow the latter procedure, and bring the shot off, you are supplied with a very simple problem to solve with stroke number two; but the question always arises—Is the risk of disaster worth the possibilities of gain? And it is in this respect that one is able to realise the merits of the Prestwick course. I have quoted the first hole as an example simply for the reason that it is the first hole; but at many of the holes at Prestwick the player has to tax his brains as to whether he should play a free, open game—the game of nature—or attempt the feat of arriving at the holeside with a minimum risk of danger, a course which may make the approach more difficult, but in the end may be the safer method of campaign.

As another instance, may be quoted the third hole. It is a distinct advantage to place your tee shot close to "The Cardinal," as you can then either get home in two or else get very nearly home, and the nearer you are to that green with your second shot the better for you. Again, at the fourth hole you are in the position that you can either play for safety to the left or else you can take a comparatively direct line and stand the chance of going out of bounds. It is a species of shot in the playing of which, before you hit the ball, you have to make up your mind definitely: half measures are no use—they always end in disaster. And this happens at many of the holes on the course. Occasionally there are tee shots which one can "lace into" with impunity, but there are few at which it is not necessary to use the discrimination of discretion.

If Prestwick has a fault, it lies in the formation of the ground around the putting greens, as it often occurs that when two players have played almost equally good shots, one of them has to play an approach which it is almost impossible to keep dead, whilst player number two, if he hits the ball at all truly, cannot help finishing very near the hole indeed. This is very noticeable at the third hole. If with your second shot you are sufficiently well placed on the left-hand side to strike the species of gutter which runs up to the hole, the playing of shot number three resolves itself into a mere question of gauging the strength of the stroke, for, with regard to the question of direction, the ball must eventually remain near the hole. But if you are too much to the left or at all to the right, the successful playing of the shot is almost as much a question of chance as a question of ability—anything may happen. Again, this same state of affairs is to be found at the thirteenth hole. From the left the hole is comparatively easy to approach, but from the right the element of chance enters very much into the argument. You may play the shot absolutely correctly, and one rub of adverse fortune will result in the ball finishing yards away from the hole. Of course, the moral reads: always keep to the left, whence you are able to play an easy approach; but the lies or the stances for the playing of this second shot are not always of the best: in fact, they are often very awkward and difficult to manage, and in them lies the history of so many indifferent seconds at this hole. If there is a hole in the world of golf which has been first freely and secondly adversely criticised, it is the fifteenth hole at Prestwick. Everyone who is not associated with the Prestwick course, be it from sentimental or other points of view, invariably asks the question, "Why is that bunker right in the middle of the course, say, some 180 to 185 yards from the tee?" The reply invariably is, "Oh, to make you play with your head;" but the reply generally comes from players who can never reach this bunker except under the most favourable of conditions, and, in consequence, for 300 of the 365 days that they play are at liberty to take any risks they please, and never by any chance reach that particular hazard. In consequence, I make bold to say that they are not in a position to form a judgment. The fifteenth hole is an interesting hole, but it is nevertheless a bad hole, and I am far from alone in this opinion. But taking the Prestwick course all in all, it is the one course on which the Championship is played about which the general public say a kindly word. St. Andrews may have more ardent devotees, but all have something nice to say of Prestwick, and there is more than one man in the world who has said bitter things about the Royal and Ancient classic green.

CHAPTER XV

GENERAL DEDUCTIONS ON GREENKEEPING

By HORACE G. HUTCHINSON.

ONE of the points which comes out most strongly on a review of the contributions of the specialists in particular soils is that the profession of the modern greenkeeper is no easy one—not one to be picked up as a kind of light additional accomplishment by the caddie who has gone on to be professional player or club-maker. It is evident that to meet modern requirements it has to be made a profession of itself—that a man has to study to fit himself for it, has to possess some elementary knowledge of chemistry in order to understand the constituents of the food of grasses, and some knowledge of botany respecting the different kinds of those grasses and the conditions for their growth. It is also essential that he shall be a man of observation, and that he shall not be so fast bound in his acquired rules as to be unable to make for himself the deductions needed as he watches the different growth of grasses on different greens and in different parts of the same green, according to the exposure and the moisture-retaining power of the spot in which the particular grass is growing. In fact, if a man is to be a greenkeeper in the best modern sense, it is wise for him that he should apply himself to learning the job, as he would any other profession, under a skilled teacher—if he be fortunate enough to find one, and, if not, to do the best he can for himself with book-learning and attentive study of greens.

Perhaps there is hardly a feature which comes out of the discussion in the preceding pages with greater prominence than the unanimity with which it is recommended that worms be removed from putting greens. It is a recommendation on which I should insist strongly from what I have seen of my own experience, but had hardly expected that it would be so unanimous. The seaside courses do not suffer from worms as do the inland. I had imagined (for I had been told that it was so) that on some of the stiffest soils it was advisable to retain a certain number of worms to give circulation to air and moisture through the ground, but it hardly seems to be the case. We may take it as a result of all experience that the worm is to be removed absolutely from inland putting greens. I am sure that this is right. In himself he is of no harm, for we do not see him. What we do see are the casts which he leaves behind, and which are so useful for fertilising the soil in the absence of other fertilisation. Obviously the casts cannot be left where the worm has put them, and the operation of their removal is troublesome: it involves expensive labour. Even when most carefully done it is bound to involve some injury to grass, and when done carelessly is apt to do it grievous injury. The old plan used to be, roll the worm casts flat when they were damp, and so to make a pat of clay through which no grass could grow. We now employ better methods, brushing away the casts or breaking them up with a long bamboo rod with a thin flexible end. This is an admirable plan where it is available, because the bamboo has not the same tendency as the broom to tear up tender young grass, but it is only on a few soils that it can be used effectively all the year round. On the clay the casts become so hard in the dry weather that the foot or the hand breaking them up is by far the best way of dealing with them. I am no friend to much brushing, for it will always injure young blades, will make the blades already grown stick up and stare at you, and if always done in one direction will make the green twice as fast down the line of brushing as against it. It has been rather necessary to speak of dealing with worm casts because it is a subject that most of the specialists of the previous chapters have not tackled very closely, and, in tackling it, certainly have not done sufficient justice to the usefulness of the bamboo rod and its freedom from the bad qualities of the roller and the broom as a worm-cast dispeller.

The best way of all, however, with worm casts

is to see that there shall not be any—to use the worm-destroying liquids so often and so effectively that there shall be no worms to make casts. I see that Hunter of Deal remarks in a Jovian kind of way, "Whenever I see there are too many of them, I reduce them," and he does not regard them as a nuisance wholly to be abolished; but then Hunter is speaking of the soil of Deal, which is of the very best and lightest golfing quality, and least appreciated by the earth worm. On such soils the casts, few in number and small in size, are sandy in character, and can be easily broken up by the lightest touch of the bamboo. It is on the heavy soils that they are really a trouble, and from them the absolute banishment of the worm is to be devoutly wished.

This conclusion leads naturally to the consideration of what the specialists have to say on the subject of dressing the greens, for, of course, the worms are natural fertilisers, and if you remove them, you must do something to help the richness and aeration of the ground. Being specialists of different soils, the writers have naturally very different advice to give, according to the character of the soil that they are prescribing for. The thin soils require enrichment, but the fat soils require some refining agent, such as sea-sand. To supply the aeration, when there is a tendency for the ground to become packed too hard, rest and dressing are recommended, and, above all, raising the ground with a fork in such a way as to loosen it and to make holes in it without breaking the surface continuity of the turf. But though the specialists have their particular advice to give according to the soil that they are discussing, there is one point on which their agreement is sufficiently remarkable to be worth noting : the danger, namely, of bringing soil or natural manure from a distance, or from ground unlike in character to that on which it is to be put. Of course, this is to be understood in a rational way. If a poverty-stricken seaside green is removed by several miles from any richer soil with which it may be fattened, it is obviously impossible to feed it with any useful nutriment brought from a nearer place, but there is always a danger in this kind of enrichment, and it is best, if possible, to leave the fresh soil by itself for a year or so, to see whether it seems disposed to develop any weeds that will be bad for the putting greens, before spreading it about. Plantain is a weed particularly to be feared in natural manure or soil brought from a distance, and it seems to love to fasten on a seaside green and spread all over it. It gave the Green Committee at Westward Ho a terrible time for several years : they have only just got rid of it by the laborious process of hand-picking, just as recommended in Mr. Beale's chapter, and the majority of the judges seemed disposed to think that it had been introduced with the soil or manure brought from a distance.

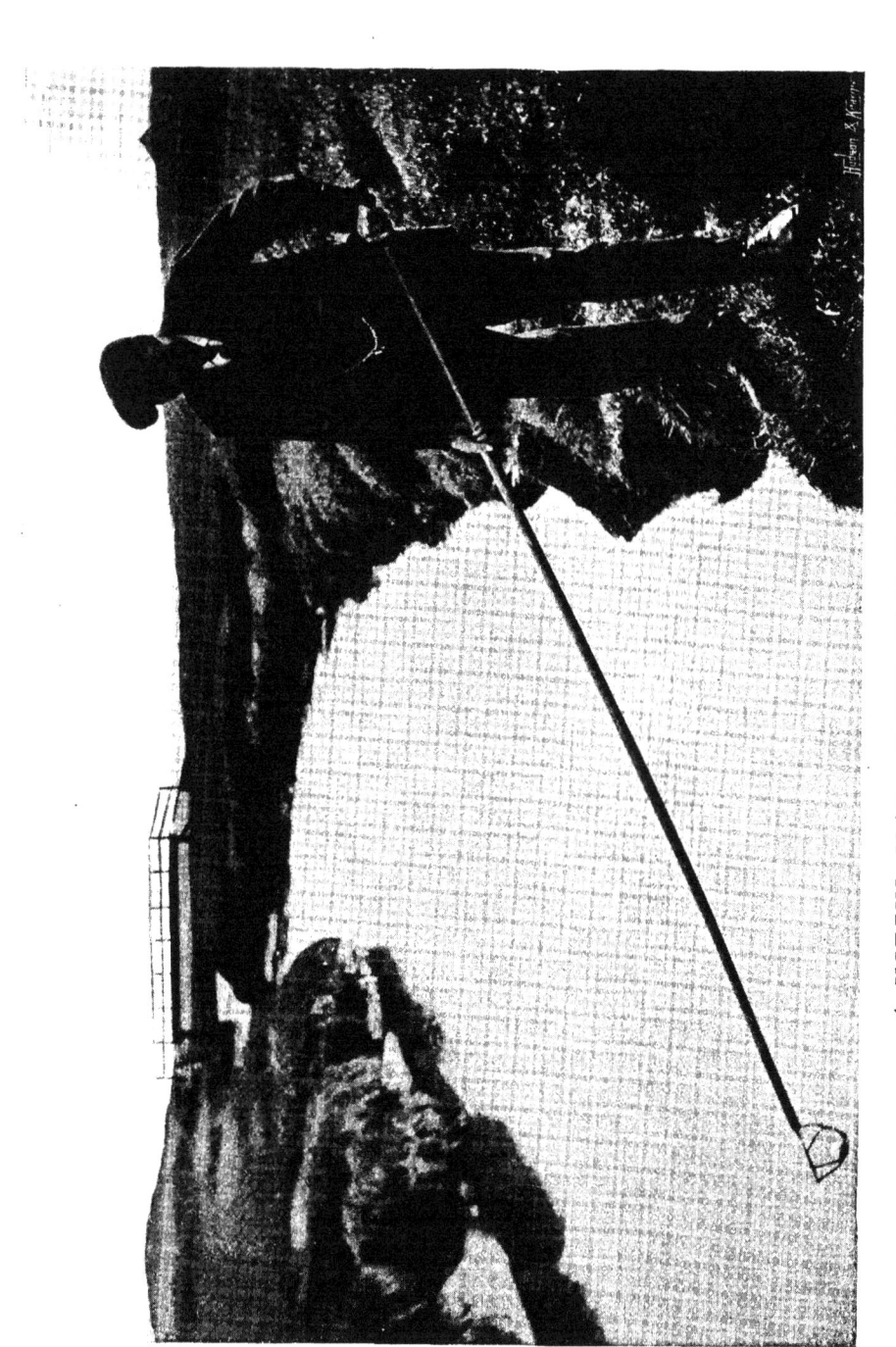

A USEFUL MAN AT THE WATER HAZARD.

CARDINAL'S NOB—PRESTWICK.

No doubt there is far less risk of introduction of ill weeds of this kind with the use of chemical manures, and the greenkeeper or some of the Green Committee should be sufficiently versed in botanical chemistry (if that is the right phrase for it) to know the constituents of plant life in which their soil is naturally deficient and the right kind of manure to use in order to supply the deficiency. Failing this knowledge in the greenkeeper or the Green Committee, or failing a sufficient confidence in it on the part of the members of the club, it is best to send for an expert who will give advice that may be trusted. It is a very invidious thing to say, and one that will not make for popularity, but it seems that of all the golfers who have contributed to this volume it is Mr. Colt that has given this very important subject the most thorough and scientific attention, though I must frankly and admiringly admit Hugh Hamilton's intimate knowledge of the use and qualities of different grasses.

It has been great fun reading the opinions of the experts, especially where they differ. On the whole, I have to confess with some little disappointment that they are in great general agreement. It is very charming, however, to read Mr. Mure Fergusson in one chapter selecting the bunkers at Walton Heath for special condemnation—" They are so deep that you cannot get out of them towards the hole, and any fool can get out sideways"—and in the next chapter Mr. C. K. Hutchison picking out these very same bunkers as examples of what bunkers should be on an inland green. It is true that he praises them with a careful reservation in the favour of those that have no rampart. The rampart he condemns. He praises them in some measure for the very quality for which Mr. Mure Fergusson condemns them. My own impression is that there is justice in the view of both witnesses, but that neither has quite *approfondi* the subject. I use the expressive French word, which is especially in place where the question is one of depth. It is a subject of which the depths never have been really explored. The deep bunker, to which Mr. Fergusson objects, is undoubtedly a bad bunker, because it reduces all men to an equality (except the very bad player, who cannot get out of a bunker at all) *when it occurs through the green.* For a bunker through the green you require a flatter affair, with irregular sides and nooks and outlets, so that a man can exercise his ingenuity and his powers of hooking and slicing and of lofting the ball, without the common or garden dig, in order to get his ball out and to send it an appreciable distance towards the hole. But, on the other hand, when the bunker is a guard to a putting green—which means that you do not want to get the ball any great distance out of it, but want to measure the force accurately—then the deep bunker is very

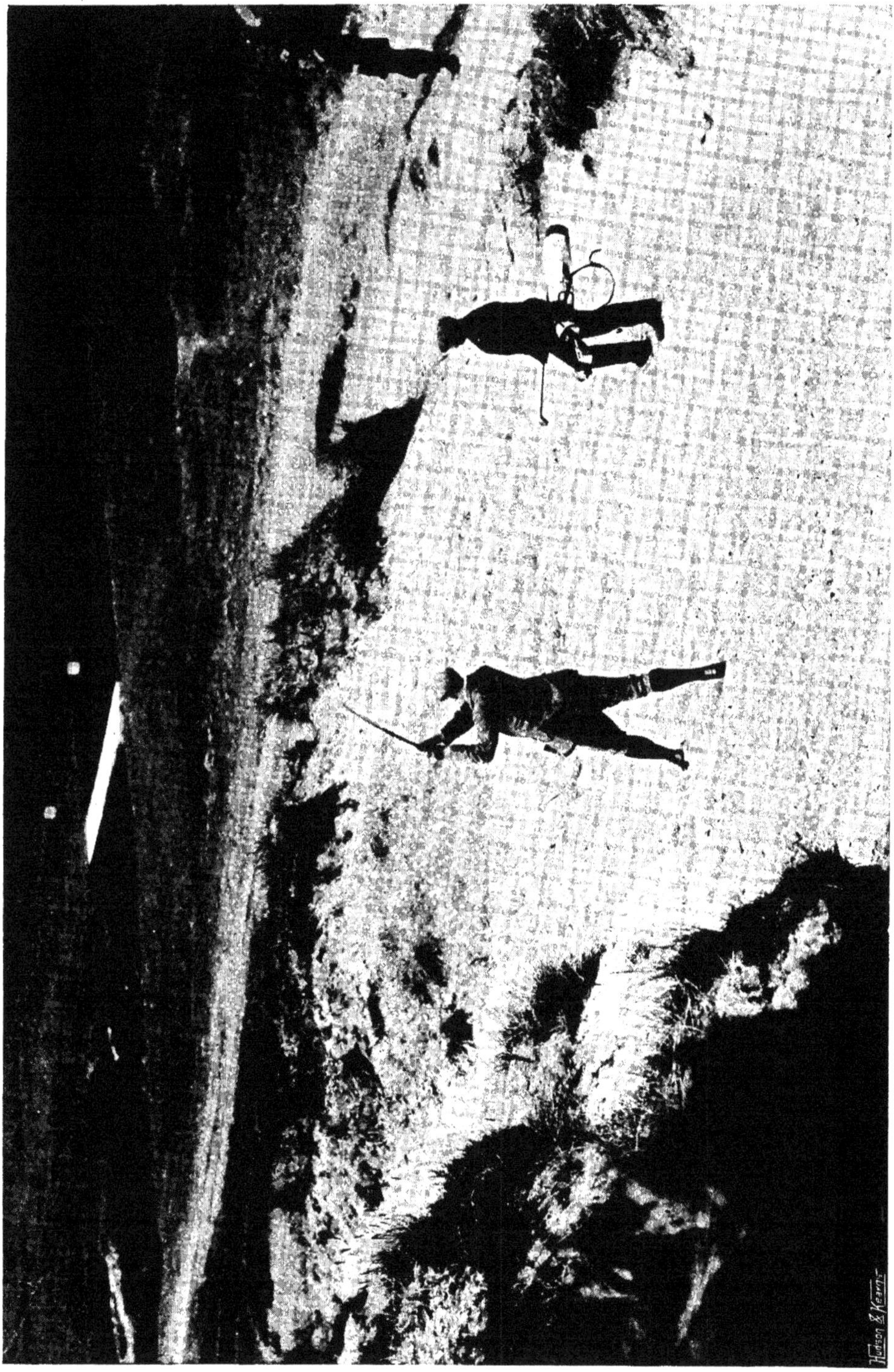
Hudson & Kearns

"HELL" AT ST. ANDREW'S.

much in its right place. These two features of sand bunkers, appropriate to different positions relatively to the hole, ought to be more discriminated than they are. We may, perhaps, take "Hell" at St. Andrews as a good example of a bunker through the green. It is irregular in form, fairly large in size, and has many outlets. Similarly, the pot bunker guarding the green at the second hole at St. Andrews may be taken as a good specimen of that kind of bunker in its right place.

There are not many inland greens which have the luck to possess a sandy subsoil, so that the questions appropriate to true sand bunkers should not apply to them. In some greens the making of a sunken bunker generally means the making of a small pond, and where the soil will not allow the water to drain readily away, and there is no such fall in the ground as suggests an easy means of draining in the ordinary way, a good recommendation is made of draining vertically, by means of a bore leading down to a porous stratum. This is an expedient which is recommended for use on putting greens also, where the water lies and there is no means of carrying it off by the natural gradient.

A difficulty on which I have been able to get no lights, though I have looked for them and have asked for them here and here of those most likely to supply them, is the difficulty of finding some floral hazard for planting on inland or on any greens. The natural golfing hazard, other than sand bunkers, seems to be "whin"—what we in the South call gorse or furze. But experience on the classic courses has sadly taught us what a poor thing the "whin" is to resist niblicks and nailed boots. St. Andrews, Prestwick, Musselburgh, and many other places of fame join in proving to us that the idea of planting whins as a floral hazard would be vanity of vanities, since those that have been long established are soon worn away to nothing. I think that Mr. Fowler in his chapter, which is really descriptive of the methods practised at Walton Heath, gives a good indication of the right way of dealing with the potential floral hazard that is found ready grown when we come to the laying out of heath courses. What he does —and I advised the same at Le Touquet with regard to the long grass and bushes—is to leave a margin in front of the tee, say, a hundred yards or more in width, to catch and to punish a topped drive, and to leave similar margins—of course, not nearly so wide—at each side of the mown and well-kept sward, between the "pretty," as modern people are in the fashion of calling it, and the "ugly" original jungle. But in leaving this, it is well to scythe it down to such a moderate height that it will not be the occasion of innumerable lost balls and infinite delay. This is comment which may apply to all sorts of the floral hazards which you may find ready to hand—to "whin," heather, and mere long tussocky grass. Incidentally, I may observe that, in my humble judgment, the value of tussocky, grass as a hazard has been immensely underrated. It is not magnificent in aspect, but it is very enduring, both because of its toughness and of its capacity for quick recuperation; and as for its capacity for giving golfing punishment, that will not be questioned by anyone who took part in the Amateur Championship in the year of Mr. Travis, the demon putter, at Sandwich. The grass on the two sides of the course at that time was almost as bad as "whins." Leaving your grass long, for hazards, is a doctrine which ought to be considered a great deal more attentively than it is, and probably our nurserymen could give some grass seed which would produce the tussocky kind which seems best for the purpose. For the rest, as regards hazards, the nurserymen have failed me. I have asked many what is the right thing to plant. There are suggestions, of course, such as buckthorn, juniper, heather, and even the "whin," which the golfer has so thoroughly proved to be wanting in some of the most necessary qualities. I am rather driven back to the conclusion that for a side hazard of the floral kind the tree, probably the Scottish fir, is the best thing that can be planted when you have done all that may be done with the natural floral growths. You must surround this with a paling at first, for protection, and make people drop outside, with a penalty, until the trees have grown stout enough in the trunk to take care of themselves, and, once you have established them, they will remain. Of course, people will tell you that trees are "not golfing hazards." They would be puzzled to explain what they suppose themselves to mean by phrases of the kind. Presumably a railway line with all its amenities is not a natural product of the links, yet it has been a "golfing hazard" at St. Andrews for a number of years, which seems to have sanctified it. But if you will regard such a tree hazard as that at the fifteenth hole at New Zealand, you will not fail to find that trees are able to make a very fine hazard indeed. They stretch out, a tall row of firs, across the direct line to the hole. You may take your choice of alternatives—over or, with a slice, round. And that in itself is good, that you should have this alternative, so as to exercise your divine intelligence. There is no chance of niblicking the trees down, like the whins. They will out-last your golfing days.

The manner in which they come out into the course, across the direct line and yet permitting a flanking movement, with a slice on to the direct course, brings us into touch with the question, much mooted in some of the previous chapters, as to the desirability of having any hazards right across the course. The fashion of the first inland hazards, made in the beginning of the golf boom

—straight ditches and "cops" across the course, one for the tee shot to carry and one just before the hole—has been very justly condemned. In that righteous condemnation there was a tendency to go to the other extreme—to say that no hazard ever ought to extend across the course, that there should always be a way to slice, or to pull, or to putt round. The final conclusion of the present-day golfer seems to be a little more moderate. The cross hazards are condemned as a rule. They are to be the exception. But without them a man is hardly taught to use his mashie at all, or to loft up to the hole, and drop dead, with any club. One of the most beautiful strokes in the game is permitted to be lost to it. A few of the right-across-the-course hazards I certainly think there ought to be, though not of the straight "cop" kind. But on this general subject I shall say a few more words in the last chapter; and since the subject was introduced by the floral hazard, it may be well to say that the tree kind of floral hazard does not seem as well adapted for across-the-course hazards as for a side hazard. I think there ought to be a way round, and for this reason: trees, to drive over, imply that the shot must be played very high—high enough to surmount them, at all events—and this further implies a shot that is quite likely to be an impossible one if there is a gale of wind against the player. It seems to me that for this reason there ought always to be a way round any hazard which is of a great height.

On the question of applying water to putting greens, there seems to be some little difference of opinion. Different soils, different aspects on the same soil, and different gradients require different treatment in this respect as in others. The intelligence of the greenkeeper has to be constantly alert. But if water is to be applied at all, there is a consensus of opinion about the right way of applying it—through a sprinkler, so that it shall be water in an ærated condition (as it is called, though I expect that is only another and less simple way of saying, in small drops), as like rain as can be produced artificially. And the night is the best time for its application. On this there is no division of opinion, neither is it disputed that to water in bright sunshine is fatal and foolish.

The rolling and the mowing questions must be left to be considered in their special connection with special characters of grass and soil. A hint of Mr. Colt's will be observed, because it is a hint that few would have the courage to give: it is the suggestion that where there is a difficulty about getting a good green of grass the small white clover might well be tried, for a while at least, to make a green. But he is insistent that attention should be paid to its being clover of this particular kind: he especially guards himself against being thought to say a word in favour of the clovers generally, in preference to grass, or even as a tolerable substitute for them.

In conclusion, it would, no doubt, be too much to expect that these contributions contain the final wisdom that will ultimately be reached on the subject of greenkeeping. It is not to be desired that they should. But what is to be hoped, and even to be asserted, is that they have advanced the problem a long step towards better solution by their collection into this convenient space, and have considerably simplified them for the greenkeeper's future service.

CHAPTER XVI

A FEW LEADING PRINCIPLES IN LAYING OUT LINKS

By Horace G. Hutchinson

THERE are certain points, some of which are emphasised in the previous chapters, and others which have been passed over without quite the emphasis which they deserve, that may now be commended briefly to the notice of all who are studying to lay out a golf course to the best advantage. As a rule, courses in the past have been laid out in too haphazard a manner, without, as it would seem, a sufficient study and knowledge of first principles.

The first "first principle" on which I should like to lay emphasis is of the negative kind, but I do not think one can be too positive in insistence on it. It is that there should be no blind approach shots—not one. I do not say that there should be no "blind" shots—though any large number of them is very much to be deprecated—but certainly there should be no "blind" approach shots. The reason that there should be this distinction drawn is that the approach stroke, as its very name implies, is, or should be, a stroke of much accuracy. It is a stroke which has, as its reasonable object, to put the ball so near the hole as to give a chance of holing it out with the next shot. For this purpose you want to see the flag, and you want to see the whole of the flag, including the part of the stick where it rises above the ground. The hole is still a "blind" hole, virtually, even though you may be able to see the bunting of the flag. The bunting does not tell you how far distant the hole is. It does not enlighten you on that point within twenty yards. It is a mere direction guide. The reason that one would allow a few, but only a few, "blind" holes, if they were to be reached by a long shot, is that there is a pleasure in the variety which they afford. The tee shot over "The Himalayas" at Prestwick and the second shot to the seventeenth hole on the same course are examples. Playing a full shot to a hole you do not aim with the same accuracy as with the approach stroke. It is less important to know whether the hole is ten yards nearer or ten yards farther. So the blindness can be excused for the sake of the interesting variety of the shot in the one case; it is not to be excused at all on an ideal course in the case of an approach shot.

A second principle which may be laid down for the ideal course is that there shall be no bunker right across the course except in a one-shot hole. The reason of this is that if you have a bunker of this kind for the tee shot, unless at a hole which can be reached from the tee in any reasonable wind, you will have to put it either so far away from the tee that, with the wind against, an ordinary man cannot carry it, or else, to avoid this, so near the tee that it has no interest at all unless the wind be against. If the question is of a bunker for the second shot, then, if you bring this bunker right across the course it will be either so far distant that with the wind against and the ground dead (so that the tee shot gets no run) an ordinary driver will not be able to carry it in two, or else so near that with the wind behind and keen ground the same man will drive into it. In no case, therefore, except where the hole can be reached from the tee, should you have a bunker right across the course, but in that case the bunker, though so near the tee that it can always be carried, will have sufficient interest from its nearness to the hole.

As a third among the principles which ought to be recognised, I would claim the value of the diagonal bunker. By the diagonal bunker I wish to indicate a bunker running from the edge of the green—its cliff actually forming the limit of the green—at one end, and thence coming nearly across the course in a diagonal way. An instance of this kind of bunker is the bunker before "The Redan" hole at North Berwick. The special value of a bunker of this description lies in the fact that the golfer can get nearer to the hole just in proportion as he has the courage to take more of the bunker with his carry, or, again, as he has the skill to play a pulled shot, so as to carry the near portion of the bunker and run on towards the hole. It is very obvious that this disposition of a bunker can be varied, conversely, so that its right-hand extremity forms the edge of the green, and it may run across the course diagonally towards the left hand of a man looking towards the hole from the tee. In this case, while equally giving value to the courage of the man who plays straight for the hole, the skilful slicer may arrive at the same desirable conclusion, that is to say, the vicinity of the hole; but since it always seems to me that the pulled shot, when it is desired to pull it, is a more artistic performance than the sliced shot, therefore I think that the diagonal bunker so running as to call for a pull is the better of the two, but one of each kind is not, in my humble judgment, out of place on the ideal links. In the same way, one might lay it down almost as a fourth principle that there should be two holes of the "dog-leg" or round-the-corner kind, and that the corner should obtrude itself in the one hole on the left and in the other on the right hand of the course, to provide for a pull or for a slice. Of the "dog-leg" kind is the first hole at Hoylake, an excellent hole, but one that would be better if it came a little later in the round. It is a cruel hole to start off with. The fifteenth at New

Zealand is a similar hole. Both are examples of holes where you have to go round a corner which lies on the right of the course. They are what you may call "dog-leg" holes for the slice. It is easy to imagine similar holes for the pull. These "dog-leg" holes should be two-shot holes—I do not think they make good one-shot holes; and I do not think that "out of bounds"—as the corner of the field is at the first hole at Hoylake—makes a good golfing hazard: but you want your hazard at a hole of this character to carry a severe punishment, because otherwise people will attempt, or will achieve without attempting it, a straight short cut, and will not pay the proper penalty. It is to be noted that the obtruding corners both of the "dog-leg" holes hazard and the diagonal bunker principle are to be associated with the ordinary bunkers guarding the hole, and so on. They are not meant to preclude the others, or to exclude them.

A fifth principle that ought to be taken to heart by the landscape gardener is the value of bunkers arranged *en échelon*, that is to say, arranged like steps, with one nearer the tee than the other, or than the others, for it is possible to have two steps (that is to say, bunkers) or more. The value of this arrangement is that it gives the player the option of the alternative courses, according to his mood, to his power, and to the direction and strength of the wind. Thus, in a calm the longish driver may go to carry the

GIRL OF CALIFORNIA

A VAST SAND BUNKER.

EXAMPLE OF HAZARD FORMED BY BROKEN GROUND—18th HOLE, ASHDOWN FOREST.

bunker which is nearest; with a light wind behind he may go to carry the second farthest bunker; and with a strong wind he may go for the third. The third, therefore, presuming that there are more than two steps, ought obviously to lie the most directly in the line to the hole, or, if not that, ought at least to give to the man who carries it an advantage in the shape of giving him an easier second shot, for if it does not give him some such advantage there is no inducement for him to attempt the carry. If the wind be against, so that the player cannot carry the nearest bunker, this arrangement gives him a place to play for—he can play short of the farthest bunker. The arrangement can be further varied by having two steps, or bunkers, one on either side of the course, and running out into it, and a third in the middle of the course. This third bunker may be either nearer to the tee than the others, so that a good drive on a calm day would carry it, though such a drive would not carry either of the side bunkers, or it may be farther away than the others, in which case these others should be at such distance that on a calm day a good shot can carry them.

A sixth principle, which the layer out of courses should always have in mind, but which is more in evidence in some holes than in others, is that he should give the accurate driver the just value for a correctly placed tee shot.

should not be merely a question of straightness and accuracy putting a man nearer the hole than inaccuracy: it should also, at one or two holes in the round at all events, give him a distinctly easier, as well as a shorter, stroke to play. With this principle is bound up the principle of punishing inaccuracy, not only by getting into hazards, but by getting into less favourable undulations of ground. This is a principle which is well illustrated at the hole which is called "Perfection" at North Berwick. It is a hole which falls a little short of the ideal of its name, because the second shot is "blind" and not quite long enough, but the tee shot is as nearly as possible ideal for the value which it gives to an absolutely correct tee shot. There is a kind of fan-shaped plateau, with the angle of the fan towards the tee, on which the ball lies fairly. On the one side are sandhills, and beyond them the sea, and on the other is ground at a lower level than the plateau, with bad, irregular lies from which it is very difficult to get the ball to the green. This fan-wise shape of the fair-lying ground is precisely what it should be—the longer the shot the more room it should have, for an error in initial direction which causes a twenty yards divergence at a hundred yards causes an [forty] yards at two hundred from the [po]int. For this reason the good lying [oug]ht to increase in width, for a full tee [at t]he distance from the tee, instead of diminishing, like the neck of a bottle, as it is often seen to do. This principle of penalising inaccuracy by the conformation of the ground may be employed very well in a one-shot hole, a crooked shot or a short shot being liable to be kicked aside to ground from which the approach to the hole is difficult, but the straight and long shot carrying to a fairly broad plateau on which the ball may run up to the green.

Of course these first principles of laying out a course may be used in combination one with another. We may have a tee shot over bunkers *en échelon* or on to a fan-shaped fair-lying place followed by a diagonal bunker for the second shot, and so on, and you will always remember that you may have your green much more closely guarded by bunkers if it is to be approached by a short shot than by a long one. Also, it is to be remembered that if you have a bunker across the course in a one-shot hole it may be placed a great deal nearer the green if the green be at an incline towards the tee and if it be a heavy green, than if it be a flat and keen green. These are truths so obvious that they are almost truisms, but truisms have been defined as the truths which are most easily forgotten, and we find plenty of illustration of the aptness of that definition in the laying out of many a golf course. There are some who will tell you that there should never be a bunker beyond the hole, because it encourages short and timorous approaching, but I do no altogether hold with them, for though one does not want to penalise boldness, still it is not very artistic work to go banging right beyond the hole in the happy certainty that no hazard awaits the ball so played.

Armed with these first principles and with all the rest of the wisdom contained in this remarkable book, you may proceed cheerfully to the laying out of the ideal links.

I do not think that anyone will do wisely who proceeds to such a task and despises the object lessons which he may find ready·prepared for him. I mean that he will, if he be a wise man, consider the features of the best holes already extant, and try to embody them, with any improvements which his ingenuity may suggest, in his new green. There is no other short hole quite as good, so far as I am aware, as the " Short Hole Coming In" at St. Andrews. It is of a sound length, it is very shrewdly guarded, you see the ground all the way, including the hole itself. If it have a fault, it is that the bunker on the left, which punishes a pull, inflicts too severe a penalty. It would be better if it were not quite so bad, quite so deep, with quite such a sheer and high cliff. In my humble judgment it is well to have two short holes on your course, balanced by ong ones, of more than two full-shot neasured by the length of shot with ed balls); and, besides the two short ink that you might have as many as two more which can be just reached from the tee. It need not be thought that this implies a shortness of the whole course. Hoylake is, I believe, the longest of all the Championship courses, yet it has four holes which can be reached in one, even when it is at full stretch. I have spoken of the merit of "dog-leg" holes, of which I would advise that there should be two, and with regard to an object lesson for the long holes, that is to say, those which are more than two-shot holes, it seems as if we must come again to St. Andrews to look for it. If there is a better three-shot hole than the "Long Hole Coming In" at St. Andrews I do not know it, with the tee shot between the "Beardies" and the wall, the second away to the left, short of "Hell," or straight along the "Elysian Fields," if the wind be against, and then the shot home. But if the ideal is desired, then I would say let the face of the plateau on which the hole is placed be made less abrupt, so that a ball will run up it, if played at the right strength, and let the green be made rather bigger. That is all that is wanting to make it perfection. I think it will be generally conceded that this is a very fine three-shot hole. I will also mention another, about which there will be no such consensus of opinion—it is the seventeenth, much reviled hole at St. Andrews. This hole is reviled because its green is so cruelly guarded, by the pot bunker on one side and the road on the other. If, when the ground is keen and the wind not against, a man tries to get on this green in two, he is almost sure to pay the penalty, but if he plays his second, as he should, well away to the right, then, if both first and second have been long and well placed, he will have an open approach to a green which is narrow enough, but of which he will have all the length to play at.

Second-shot holes of a fine class are many. Two very good ones, according to my view, are the seventeenth at Prestwick and the sixteenth at Littlestone. Both, it is to be admitted, fail of the ideal perfection, if only because both are "blind"; but in both cases it is the kind of "blindness" which does not much matter, because both are approached with full shots—that is to say, if properly played by a good driver on a good day. The seventeenth at Prestwick would, however, be improved if the bunker guarding the green were on the side of the hill on which it would be visible as one approached the hole, instead of on the side on which it is unseen. For the rest, good two-shot holes are so many that further selection would be invidious.

It is no use being an editor unless you can have the last word as well as the first, and my last word is that the man who lays out courses should lay to his heart these first principles. I am all for Mr. Hilton's suggestion that the places for the short holes ought to be the first consideration. The properly guarded greens for them are such as you must find, so far as can be, naturally provided, because they are the most difficult to create by art. It is not always possible to apply these first principles, but they must be the ideal to be borne in mind, and applied as far as practicable. An ideal which is limited by the practical is hardly worth having.

THIS BOOK IS DUE ON THE LAST DATE STAMPED BELOW

AN INITIAL FINE OF 25 CENTS
WILL BE ASSESSED FOR FAILURE TO RETURN THIS BOOK ON THE DATE DUE. THE PENALTY WILL INCREASE TO 50 CENTS ON THE FOURTH DAY AND TO $1.00 ON THE SEVENTH DAY OVERDUE.

MAR 4 1946	REC'D LD
MAR 26 1947	MAY 1959
25Apr'50HJA	7May'68SL
24Nov'53DD	LD
1-17-53	1963
UCLA INTER-LIBRARY LOAN DEC 8 1958 14 DAYS AFTER RECEIPT	
8Dec'54SE	
26May'59KK	
	LD 21–100m-7,'40(6936s)

Lightning Source UK Ltd.
Milton Keynes UK
UKHW020707201118
332647UK00009B/270/P